The Immediacy of God

The Immediacy of God

Douglas Vickers

WIPF & STOCK · Eugene, Oregon

THE IMMEDIACY OF GOD

Copyright © 2009 Douglas Vickers. All rights reserved. Except for brief quotations in critical publications or reviews, no part of this book may be reproduced in any manner without prior written permission from the publisher. Write: Permissions, Wipf and Stock Publishers, 199 W. 8th Ave., Suite 3, Eugene, OR 97401.

Wipf & Stock
A Division of Wipf and Stock Publishers
199 W. 8th Ave., Suite 3
Eugene, OR 97401
www.wipfandstock.com

ISBN 13: 978-1-60608-625-4

Manufactured in the U.S.A.

Scripture quotations are from the King James Version

To
ANN
With gratitude

Contents

Preface ix

PART ONE FOUNDATIONS

1 Preliminary Considerations 3

2 The Immediacy of God 17

3 The Immediate Imputation of Sin 42

4 The Immediate Imputation of Righteousness 61

5 Immediacy in Sanctification 82

PART TWO APPLICATIONS

Introduction to Part Two 99

6 The Christian Mind and the Mind of Christ 101

7 The Justification of Christ? 122

8 Adoption and the Paradox of Faith 145

Bibliography 165

Preface

My objective in this book is to bring into prominence some aspects of the doctrines of God and salvation, of theology and soteriology, and to view them under the perspective of what I have referred to as the immediacy of God. When I adduce the idea of immediacy I do not refer primarily to the possibility that certain outcomes and events might be, in a temporal sense, the immediate result of their cause. Instances of such a time reference will be observed. But my principal concern, that motivates the argument I shall advance, is with the fact that certain actions of God are immediate, rather than mediate, in the sense that no mediating entity or cause exists between the action and the resulting effects on human nature and the human condition.

After a consideration of the apologetic foundations and the hermeneutical principle against which the argument proceeds, I address the immediacy of God in his being, his knowledge, and his will, and reflect on the independency of God of any cause, will, or possibility external to himself. In the light of conclusions reached on those levels, I raise such questions as the following: Are we properly to understand the imputation to his posterity of the guilt of Adam's sin as an immediate or a mediate imputation? If we were to opt for the latter, what, then, would be the mediating element or cause? Are we to say that the imputation to the sinner of the righteousness of Christ is immediate or mediate? Or what of regeneration? Could it be said that any mediating cause, such, perhaps, as the reason and will of the individual person, properly fulfills such a mediating function? We shall see that some theologies do, in fact, claim to that effect.

While the intent of the work is to examine in a fresh way the doctrinal outworking of the principle of immediacy, at several points it engages relevant contemporary theological debates. The scope of the book is set out more fully in the first chapter, and the introduction to Part Two indicates my concern for the relation between doctrine and application in the Christian life. Chapters 6 and 8 reproduce the substance of papers delivered at the 2008 meetings of the New England Reformed Fellowship (NERF) and the Reformed Congregational Fellowship (RCF) respectively, and I thank the organizing committees of NERF and RCF for the courtesies accorded me on those occasions.

I should be sailing under false colors if I allowed it to be thought that I claim originality for every argument and conclusion in the chapters that follow. Informed readers will recognize that I am heavily indebted to a long line of theologians in the Reformed tradition, and I have endeavored to acknowledge my indebtedness throughout the work. But as every scholar-author knows, it is frequently impossible to identify where and when, in the course of work over the years, ideas and conclusions were gathered and became part of one's own well-formed attitudes and structures of thought.

I happily record a special indebtedness to Ann Hopkins, whose editorial assistance over more years than it might be judicious to mention has been of immense help in the writing of many books and professional papers. From my first book to the present, when in the winter of the years the days are shorter and the shadows longer, Ann's sage advice and professional skill in all things literary have been an invaluable support. I dedicate this book to her as a token of gratitude and esteem.

For infelicities of argument that remain I take full responsibility.

Part One
Foundations

1

Preliminary Considerations

THE SHIFTING COMPLEXITIES OF our time challenge the assertion of meaning. That challenge arises from the fact that no metanarrative, no locus of explanatory bedrock, stands behind the clamoring relativities from which interpretative standards have been evacuated. Explanation has become tenaciously individualized. Every individual, it is now thought appropriate to say, can be intellectually comfortable in his own truth. But it is a commonplace to say, a truth itself worn down to cliché, that where that is the case the danger exists that truth and falsehood are no longer distinguishable. No longer are there boundary lines between them. When anything can be believed, where anyone's truth has as much claim to credence and credibility as any other's truth, it can equally be said that one may as well believe nothing at all. There is then no truth. There are only truths, each in itself private and idiosyncratic. And then the pretences of relativity cloak virtual agnosticism. Standards of cognitive meaningfulness no longer obtain or have any claim to relevance. It is as though the lament of the author of the book of Judges has come to apply on the levels of meaning, knowledge, and interpretation as on that of ethics, "[E]very man did that which was right in his own eyes" (Judg 21:25). In action and choice, principle and pragmatism are too easily at odds, and moral murkiness becomes the servant of convenience and expediency.

By metanarrative, or what it is that stands behind the particular and shifting narratives of human explanation, is meant some overarching set of explanatory propositions from which truth in its varying instances and applications radiates. In an earlier age a theological metanarrative guided judgment and opinion. It resided in the basic apologetic presupposition that *God is*. That in turn gave rise to the realization that all of the outcomes and instances of history, all of the exigencies that make up life in the large and in the smallness of everyday, are what they are because of God's instantiation of his covenantal purpose and objectives. God's being and God's covenant provided the foundation for human understanding. In short, as the awareness that *God is* provided a basic apologetic presupposition, so a fundamental hermeneutical principle, or principle of interpretation, was discovered in God's covenantal design and faithfulness. But contemporary opinion, even, unfortunately, contemporary theological opinion, appears to have fairly completely surrendered such reliable moorings. The basic apologetic presupposition and the fundamental hermeneutical principle are correlative in their impact and effects.

APOLOGETIC PRESUPPOSITION

Consider for the moment the question of apologetics. We may conjure within the scope of that not only theological apologetics as a basis for ongoing doctrinal formation, but the apologetical understanding or explanatory foundation of all historical eventuation. I have referred, as a basic apologetic presupposition, to the fact that *God is*. What, then, is it possible to know of God? Or is it possible to know God? If the presupposition that *God is* is excogitated merely from within the human consciousness, if it is, that is to say, a bare intellectual presupposition, then the god who is presupposed is nothing more than an entity made in man's own image. In other words, God as he exists is not knowable merely as the end of a process of autonomous human reasoning. He does not exist at the end of a logical syllogism. God is not knowable because we have conjured God. God is knowable and known because he has revealed himself. The chain of disclosure runs from God to man, not from man to God. God is known because he has spoken, because in real time and real history he has made a self-disclosure. Meaning resides, not in what we ask about God or imagine we can discover about God, but in what God has said to us.

In our apologetic we are therefore not free to choose our presuppositions, to select them from a range of possibilities to form the basis of on-going argument and investigation. Against the claims we are making it might be held, as in the context of contemporary postmodernist thought, that one's presuppositions are necessarily private, idiosyncratic, and formed against the background of his own complex of ideas, history, and culture. If such were the case, one would be locked in what Noel Weeks has discussed as the hermeneutical circle. "He will naturally read those ideas into what he reads.... He reads out of the Bible what he reads into it."[1] There is a sense, of course, in which "We all read Scripture within a hermeneutical circle, as do all readers whether consciously or unwittingly."[2] But the question at issue is that of the source and the formation of the presuppositions that we hold as a guide to our investigations. Those presuppositions may be derived from the dogma of the church or from the confessional statements of the church, particularly, perhaps, the post-Reformation confessions of the sixteenth and seventeenth centuries. But with no freedom to choose autonomously, and with creaturely submission, the presuppositions that lead to the discovery of truth are themselves inherent in God's statement to us, as is the substance of what he has revealed. Rationalism cannot displace revelation, either at the beginning or within the process of investigation.

In his self-disclosure, as it was made, for example, to Moses of old, God said "I am that I am" (Exod 3:14). He is the self-referential God, than whom no higher law or entity or canon or possibility external to himself exists. He could not be subject to any such reality external to himself. To imagine to the contrary would be to conceive of a god lower than the God who has revealed himself in the ways the Scriptures declare. The God who has revealed himself is the God who spoke into existence all reality external to the Godhead. That reality is therefore his property. He disposes of it and does with it what he wills. It is clear that what he wills is informed by his love, and that what he has done and continues to do communicates an eternally wise purpose. The *God who is* is transcendent above all that he has made, as he is immanent in preserving and ordering all that eventuates within it.

It follows that all the facts of the universe, and all of the items and instances of eventuation within the universe, are God's facts and God's occurrences. He has, moreover, preinterpreted them for our apprehension, in that he has directed us in his Word how we are to think his thoughts after him. On another level, there are no brute facts that form basic epistemological data. On the level of our understanding, it is the meaning of the fact that gives it its factness. To grasp the point, consider what has to be regarded as the watershed of all of history, the death of Jesus Christ on the cross. What, we may ask, is the fact that is observable there? The fact

---

1. Weeks, *Sufficiency of Scripture*, 81.
2. Arand, "The Church's Dogma and Biblical Theology," 18.

for some was that there a criminal, a charlatan, a deceiver and blasphemer was receiving what he rightly deserved. But for others the fact was that there the Son of God was dying in the place of sinners. What, then, are we to say was the fact of Calvary? And similarly, God in his revelation has conveyed to us not bare or uninterpreted facts, but also the meaning of the facts. It is that that establishes their facticity. By the same token, all of the observable facts that come within the orbit of human cognition are to be recognized as God's facts, and are to be interpreted in terms of the discoverable relations they sustain to the revealed purposes of God. If the hairs on our heads are numbered, if he knows even a sparrow that falls to the ground (Matt 10:29–30), can any other occurrence in our world be unknown to him? Can a limit be proposed to his ordination and will?

The God who has spoken in actions and words of self-disclosure exists in an eternal day, outside of the time that he created as the mode of finite existence.[3] Augustine's soliloquy on the meaning of time, a category of being that was finally for him inscrutable and incomprehensible,[4] is reflected in modern times in Paul Helm's important, if demanding, study, *Eternal God*.[5] Helm observes that "The classical Christian theologians, Augustine of Hippo, say, or Aquinas or John Calvin, each took it for granted that God exists as a timelessly eternal being. They accepted it as an axiom of Christian theology that God has no memory, and no conception of his own future, and that he does not change, although he eternally wills all changes, even becoming, when incarnate in the Son, subject to humiliation and degradation. The position at the present time among philosophers and theologians is a very different one."[6]

The Christian vision, it is true, contemplates a final access to the presence of God who inhabits eternity. But the remarkable and again incomprehensible reality is that in that eternity God will still and forever be outside of time, while the host that he redeemed by his Son will be with him *in* time. Though it is a mystery beyond our ability to penetrate, God in his eternal Godness, God as he exists in the fullness of his essence in the divine Person of his Son, is and remains outside of time, while the Son is visible throughout the eternal ages of time in the human nature he

---

3. Van Til has observed, "Time is not a moving image of the abstract notion of eternity. It is God-created as a mode of finite existence." *Systematic Theology*, 66.

4. Augustine, *Confessions*, 221.

5. Helm, *Eternal God: A Study of God without Time*.

6. Ibid., xi.

assumed to himself. In his human nature he partook of our finitude and createdness. He remains identified with us in the time-bound nature he assumed. And because in the eternal age we shall not transcend our finitude we shall live through the rolling ages of eternity with him in visible and temporal presence. We bow before the mystery.

The writer of the book of *Hebrews* has spoken of God's revelation in his summary: "God, who at sundry times and in diverse manners spake in time past unto the fathers by the prophets, hath in these last days spoken unto us by his Son" (Heb 1:1–2). The eternal Son of God came into the world to declare the Father to us. "He hath declared him" (John 1:18). Given the mystery of the perichoresis or circumincession of the Godhead, (that is, the consubstantiality of the Persons of the Trinity and their existence in one another), Christ could say when he was in this world that "I and my Father are one" (John 10:30).

That the eternal Son of God should have entered into time that he himself had created, and that he should have made himself subject to the passing of time and to temporal processes, remains a mystery that will engage our worship and contemplation throughout the eternal ages. But in him the human nature was not personalized. He was, and he remained, a divine Person. As to his personhood, whatever is to be said of the *communicatio idiomatum* is to be said not of any communication of properties between the respective divine and human natures, but of the communication of properties to his person. At the incarnation of our Lord there was, as Van Til has expressively put it, "no commingling of the eternal and the temporal."[7] We must go on to say that while our Lord possessed a full human nature, with all of the faculties of soul that connote human nature, in him that human nature was not personalized. Christ was not, that is to say, a human person. He was not a divine-human person, such that the two natures were combined in some sense that would render it impossible to say that he was either uniquely divine or uniquely human. Christ was a divine Person.[8] It is true that Christ was not monophysite (having only one nature) and not monothelite (having only one will). There was in him a divine mind and a human mind, a divine will and a human will. We bow before the mystery.

---

7. See Van Til, *Defense of the Faith*, 16–17.

8. Berkhof, in *Systematic Theology*, 321–22, observed that "the Logos assumed a human nature that was not personalized, that did not exist by itself."

But the fact that Christ has now taken his place at the right hand of the Father in the human nature that he assumed at his incarnation gives poignancy to the truth that "we have a great high priest, that is passed into the heavens . . . not an high priest which cannot be touched with the feeling of our infirmities; but was in all points tempted like as we are, yet without sin. Let us therefore come boldly unto the throne of grace, that we may obtain mercy, and find grace to help in time of need" (Heb 4:14–16). Now, in his continual discharge of his heavenly high priestly office, in his intercession and sympathy for his people, the human nature of Christ informs his recognition of their state and sufferings and necessities, because he was himself subject to all human vicissitudes in the same human nature. He knows and understands our frame (Ps 103:14).

HERMENEUTICAL PRINCIPLE

Consider what I have referred to as a basic hermeneutical principle. By that I mean a principle or a key that provides an entrance to the meaning of what God has revealed and declared, and to the meaning of the human journey and the purpose of it all under the immanent providence of God. Is there an end or purpose, some grand teleological objective in view in human existence? Or are we to say that the human journey is itself without meaning? The question at issue is whether God who is, God who has spoken his self-disclosure into our time and language, has in doing so provided a principle by which the particularities of our journey in time have meaning. Or again, are we any better or more advantaged than flotsam on a sea of chance that philosophic materialism too often takes for explanation? In short, is there any reason for being? The question is whether, and if so where and how, interpretative light is thrown on our mannishness and the reason for its being, at the same time as it illumines the relations and obligations we sustain to God from whose hands we came.

If, on the other hand, all of existence is a matter of chance, there is no point in asking our questions. Human imagination in its better moments may look to the stars and feel justified in aiming at something higher than itself. But if, at the same time as it does that it must recall the cold awareness that we came from the mud, then it relapses into the claim that finally we ourselves are simply chance entities at sea in a shoreless ocean of chance. Anything can happen. And if it does happen there is not, and cannot be, any explanation for it. For if all is chance, then human being is also an inexplicable product of chance. And in that case the attempt to define ourselves amounts only to the denial and destruction of the self. At the end of thinking, darkness looms. We ourselves then have no meaning.

But against such a possible nihilism, which amounts, as we have proposed, to the denial rather than the explanation of self, stands an interpretative principle that emanates from the revelation that God has spoken. God, that is, is a God of purpose and grace. While it is necessary to say that "his ways [are] past finding out" (Rom 11:33), while in his essence and knowledge God is incomprehensible to us, we nevertheless know that he is, that we are the creatures of his hand, and that by reason of that creaturehood we sustain inescapable obligation to him (Rom 1:18–32). Our hermeneutical principle, then, comes into concurrence with, and it exhibits an accordance and confluence with, the apologetic presupposition we have already inspected. For when we know that *God is* and that he has spoken, we see that the principle of the interpretation of meaning of all things resides precisely in the speech of God. God, that is, has declared to us the purpose for which he spoke all things into existence and, moreover, his purpose in the redemption for sinners that he has set forth in his Son.

Coming to focus as the principle of interpretation is the covenantal purpose of God. The terms of that covenant are plainly discoverable in the inscripturated revelation that God has made. We shall look in due course at its terms and at the manner and objectives of its formation. It will emerge that in the timeless eternity an intratrinitarian communication within the Godhead set forth God's covenant to preserve the universe of reality that he had established, to redeem to himself an elect body of people from out of the mass of fallen humanity, to renew the heavens and the earth, and to conduct his elected people to glory with him.

The implications of such covenantal realities press their relevance upon us. For it is in the unfolding reality and the outworking of God's covenantal statement and purposes that all occurrences within the history of reality eventuate. The apostle to the Gentiles stated quite simply, but in a way whose profound meaning it is impossible to plumb fully, that God "works all things after the counsel of his own will" (Eph 1:11). God, that is, eventuates all that comes to pass. He so supervises, orders, directs, and guides the operation of personal free wills that all that he has purposed does in fact eventuate.

That very statement, of course, contains its own mysteries and challenges that will engage us again. The meaning and competence of human free will call for investigation. But if both our apologetic presupposition and our hermeneutical principle are cogently stated and held, if their mutual relevance and the accordance between them obtain, then the final explanation of all things is discoverable in the operation of God's covenant and purpose. That is why we state that history is the instantiation of God's purposes with relation to the created reality that he has established.

The scope of that eventuation demands reflection. It would be an inadmissible shortening of perspective if we were to confine it to redemptive categories or, that is, to a narrowly soteriological compass. At issue is the respect in which *all* things, things having to do with all aspects of human life, fall within the orbit of God's command. All issues and developments within the realms of the natural and social sciences, those of the arts, technologies, economics, and demographies, necessarily come within the compass of divine ordination. All things find their final explanation only when their relation to the covenantal objectives of God has been investigated and clarified. Coming to prominence in such investigations is the relation between God's common grace in the preservation and development of human culture and his redemptive grace in the salvation of his people, as that latter is projected in his covenant of redemption. For as will be seen, God's common grace is projected by him into the world of reality in the service of his redeeming grace that serves, in turn, his purpose of bringing his chosen people to share eternal glory with him.

THE IMMEDIACY OF GOD

I have chosen as my title *The Immediacy of God*. "Immediacy," I shall explain, is to be taken to refer to God in both his being and his actions. But the concept of *immediacy* is itself capable of more than one referent.

Immediacy may have, first, a temporal reference. It may have to do with the relation between an outcome or event and its causation. The effect of a causal action may occur immediately on the instigation of the act. That is in fact observable within the scope of God's redemptive acts. As we shall see more fully, the creation of new life within a sinner, the action of the Spirit of God on and within the soul of an individual that is referred to doctrinally as regeneration, produces an immediate effect. When that remarkable action of God is explored more fully it will be seen that the

Spirit of God may perform many acts on and within the soul which nevertheless are not consummated by the conveyance to the soul of the grace of regeneration. But the action of regeneration itself, when in the divine providence and the Spirit's implementation it occurs, is immediate. That action of God is referred to in the apostle's letter to the Corinthian church as having an immediate effect comparable to God's first act of creation, his speaking the universe of reality into existence. "God who commanded the light to shine out of darkness," Paul states, adverting to the first creative act, "hath shined in our hearts to give the light of the knowledge of the glory of God in the face of Jesus Christ" (2 Cor 4:6). "He [God] spoke and it was done" (Ps 33:9).

But while instances of immediate causation in a temporal sense will engage us in what follows, the concept of *immediacy* will more frequently be explored as the antonym of *mediacy*. The negating prefix "im" will bring to prominence in our thought the fact that certain actions of God, and certain resulting effects in and on the human consciousness, are *immediate* in the sense that there does not exist any mediating cause, or secondary cause, between God's action and the effect or outcome in human life and experience. An example at this early stage may be useful.

In the matter of the regeneration of an individual, to take the instance to which we have just referred, there does not exist and come into play any mediating instrument or secondary cause between the action of the Spirit of God and the effect on the soul. In some theologies, in what is known as Arminianism, for example, there is deemed to exist such a mediating secondary cause. It is argued in that scheme of things that the reason and the will of the individual stand between the call to the sinner and the possible effect in the renewal of the soul. The grace of God may come to the sinner, an Arminian says, but the decision on the sinner's part as to whether the divine overture of grace will be accepted or rejected rests within the individual will. The misconception regarding individual free will at that point implies the doctrinal error that the individual person is free in every sense to say "yes" or "no" to God. In that case the sovereignty of God in salvation has been displaced by the sovereignty of the individual. Clearly, the relations involved at such a point require extended exploration.

Further instances of *immediate* as distinct from *mediate* causation will call for discussion. In the case just referred to, the reason and will of the individual are together improperly understood as the mediating cause. Similar instances of claims to mediating causes will arise. In each case the objective of discussion will be the protection of an important and relevant doctrine of the Christian faith, or, that is, the clarification of the content of God's disclosures. To take briefly as an example, a highly significant issue and a prominent aspect of God's dealings with individuals will be seen as having to do with the imputation of the guilt of Adam's first sin to all those descending from him by ordinary generation. Imputation means simply placing to one's account. And it will be seen that because our first parent was established as the federal head, or the representative head, of the race that was to come from him, the guilt of his sin was placed to the account of us all. Or again, to take the important reciprocal case, the righteousness of Christ in his active and passive obedience is imputed to all those who believe on him in repentance and faith. Again the important question will arise as to whether the imputation in both of those cases, the imputation of the guilt of Adam's sin and the imputation of Christ's righteousness, is *immediate* or *mediate*.

THE WAY AHEAD

An expansive consideration of the immediacy of God must take up the relevance of the concept to both the being and the acts of God. In the following chapters, therefore, I shall raise for discussion a number of issues on both those levels.

As to God's being, immediacy raises the reality that, as Bavinck has put it, "Whatever God is he is of himself."[9] In that, we confront the aseity of God. By that it is meant that God is eternal and uncaused, or that he is self-caused, in that he is not dependent for his being on any thing or force or entity external to himself. Bavinck brings together what we have referred to as aseity and God's independence: "'Aseity' merely expresses the fact that God is self-sufficient in his *existence*; but 'independence' has a broader connotation, and indicates that God is self-sufficient in *everything*; in his existence, in his attributes, in his decrees, and in his works. . . . When God in Scripture ascribes aseity to himself, he reveals himself as absolute essence."[10]

Given the nature of God's being as he has revealed himself, the question arises of the immediacy of God's knowledge. When we speak of the knowledge of God we do not have in view firstly the knowledge that we

---

9. Bavinck, *Doctrine of God*, 144.
10. Ibid., 144–45.

might have of God (in which case the "of God" would be an objective genitive), but the knowledge that God himself possesses (a subjective genitive). We refer, then, to God's knowledge of himself, his knowledge of the external reality that he established, and his knowledge of his covenantal objectives. Recalling our earlier observation on the timelessness of God's existence, or recalling Augustine's comment, for example, on God's eternal day, we say that God knew all things in one eternal act of knowing. He did not have to wait to discover either the nature of his own being or existence or the meaning of any external fact situation. Cornelius Van Til has commented insightfully and challengingly on the questions we are now addressing. He states that "God, we have contended, is self-determinative. He has no non-being over against himself in terms of which he needs or can to any extent interpret himself. He is *omniscient*. He is omniscient because of what he is as a self-sufficient Being. On the other hand we must add that the nature of God's being requires complete exhaustive self-consciousness. *God's Being is coterminous with his self-consciousness.*"[11] And the same author goes on to speak also of God's knowledge of the world.

We may summarize at this point by saying that God's knowledge is not sequential, in that what he knows is not sequentially acquired. We in effect adverted to the same reality when we stated that God exists outside of time. He is, in his being and knowledge, eternal. If we were to introduce temporal sequentiality into the knowledge or the consciousness of God we would thereby be introducing sequentiality into the being of God. We would thereby be entangled in the problematic of what became known as process theology. Paul Helm again commented on the point: "[T]here is a widespread belief among Christian thinkers who are often otherwise in disagreement that God is in time. For example, such a view is characteristic of so-called 'Process Theology', which holds not only that God is in time but that it is essential to God that he changes, that his own character matures as he experiences the love, disappointment, and frustration of his creation."[12] Van Til has commented on the point by observing that "The most effective means ever invented by men to date by which to make themselves believe that they are not creatures of God and are not sinners against God is the modern process philosophy and theology."[13] It is

---

11. Van Til, *Defense of the Faith*, 35.

12. Helm, op. cit., xi.

13. In Geehan, *Jerusalem and Athens*, 394. Similar claims regarding the being and knowledge of God in time appear in the so-called "Open Theism" theology that argues,

clear that to assume such a sequentiality of development of God's being in time or the sequentiality of his knowledge would deny the God of the Scriptures as he has revealed himself. We would thereby, moreover, as will be argued, destroy the autotheotic nature of both the Son and the Holy Spirit as Persons within the divine Godhead.

It is necessary to reflect also on the immediacy of the acts of God. By that it is meant, as has already been observed, the immediacy of the effects that God produces in his relations with individuals in the world. In many instances it will be necessary to question whether those effects are immediate or mediate, in the sense that a mediating or secondary cause may or may not intervene between the divine action and the results produced on a human level. There is to be taken into account also, of course, God's use of intermediate means in many of his actions in the world. That opens to view the mysteries of God's providence and his works whereby he effects his "most holy, wise, and powerful preserving and governing all his creatures and all their actions."[14] God has from all eternity ordained all of the means to the ends he has purposed as well as the ends themselves. It will be seen that God's ordering the affairs of his creation, including the affairs of his rational creatures, extends to his ordering of the actions referable to the exercise of human free will.

But our principal concern in what follows will be with the nature of God's working, and the manner of his working, in relation to the processes of redemption. In considering God's bringing his elect people to salvation and to the eternal glory that he has ordained, it is necessary to refer to man as he exists in fourfold state in relation to God.[15] God has dealings with man, that is, in, first, man's state of innocency as initially created; second, in the state in which he exists as a result of Adam's fall; third, in the state of salvation as a result of what we have noted as God's act of regeneration and the salvific work of his Son; and fourth, in the state of glory to which, by God's electing grace, he is destined.

To anticipate briefly at this stage, and to remain within the scope of potential human experience as has just been envisaged, we shall be concerned with the immediacy or otherwise of God's action in relation

---

as does the earlier Socinianism, that God does not know, but must wait to discover, the future. See Frame, *No Other God*, and Wright, *No Place for Sovereignty*.

14. Westminster Shorter Catechism, Question 11.

15. See the highly valuable work by the Puritan theologian, Boston, *Human Nature in its Fourfold State*.

to four pivotal stages or levels of realization. Together they take up much of what is involved in the main corpus of Christian theological doctrine. First, is the imputation of the guilt of Adam's sin to the posterity that came from him by ordinary generation to be understood as immediate or mediate? In the history of doctrinal debate answers of both immediacy and mediacy have been given. In the argument we shall advance we shall hold to the postulate of immediacy.

Second, are we to understand that the act of regeneration that the Spirit of God effects in the soul of an individual is immediate or mediate? We have already touched on that question by way of example. At issue in connection with it will be the question of the capacities of soul, the state of the cognitive and volitional faculties as they exist in the individual after, and as a result of, Adam's fall. When the entailment of sin is understood in Scriptural terms, and when the disabilities of soulish faculties implicit in that entailment are taken into account, it will emerge that the regeneration of a sinner is an act of God's Spirit in which no mediating cause or element, such as human reason or will, is or can be present and active. Regeneration, it will be seen, is a secret, sovereign, and unsolicited act of God on and within the soul. In that action, while no creation of new faculties is involved, the faculties of the soul are endowed with abilities and capacities they did not previously possess.

Third, when it is seen that salvation is due to the substitutionary life and death of Christ on the sinner's behalf, his perfect active obedience to the demands of the law of God and his taking on himself the penalty of the guilt of sinners, two questions call for address. First, what is to be said of the imputation to Christ of the guilt of sin for which he paid the penalty that was of necessity administered by the justice of God; and second, what is to be said of the imputation to the repentant individual of the righteousness of Christ? Is the latter, for example, to be understood as an immediate or a mediate imputation?

Fourth, it is to be seen that the entrance of an individual to new life in and because of Christ means not only forgiveness of sin, but also adoption into the family of God and progress in sanctification, or growth in holiness, preparatory to entrance into eternal life. That progress turns for its accomplishment and certainty on the ministry to the soul of the Holy Spirit of God. That is so because the redemptive office of the Spirit, as that office was undertaken and committed to by the third Person of the Trinity in the predeterminate council of the Godhead, is such that he applies to the individual the benefits of the redemption that Christ accomplished for him. What, then, are we to say of the salvific works of the Holy Spirit in the individual soul? It will be seen that there exist important aspects of immediacy and, at the same time, aspects of mediacy. "Work out your own salvation," the apostle stated to the Philippians, "for it is God which worketh in you both to will and to do of his good pleasure" (Phil 2:12–13).

Leaving the details to what follows, we may summarize the works of God in relation to those he ordained to be saved in terms of the apostolic conclusion, "Of him [God] are ye in Christ Jesus, who of [or by] God is made unto us wisdom, and righteousness, and sanctification, and redemption" (1 Cor 1:30). In short, the proposition to be advanced and the claim to be made is that salvation in all of its parts and in all its aspects is the work of God. He makes Christ to be wisdom against the ignorance in which the human soul stands by reason of sin, righteousness against the sinner's guilt, sanctification against his pollution, and redemption against the misery in which he would otherwise be eternally bound.[16]

But as our agenda has indicated, lying behind what is to be said of God's relations with the world and its history and the purpose of redemption is the reality, the finally incomprehensible mystery, that God who exists *outside* of time has spoken to, and guides all of the history of, rational beings whom he has created to live *within* time. Who is the God of whom we speak and before whom we do well to bow in worship? We have said that the being and knowledge of God are incomprehensible to us. Our finitude underlines the reality. But while it is not possible to possess comprehensible knowledge of God, the knowledge that he communicates to us by his grace is nevertheless true knowledge. It is analogical of the fullness of knowledge inherent in God himself. Because God has created us in his image, it is necessary to say that we are, in turn, the analogue of God as to both our being and our knowledge.

Against those questions and propositions I shall begin in the following chapter to consider the immediacy of God in his triune being and his covenantal statements.

---

16. The Puritan scholar, Flavel, made the same points in his sermon on 1 Corinthians 1:30, the first in his series on "The Method of Grace." Reprinted in *Works*, vol. 2, 15–33. See page 16.

2

The Immediacy of God

My objective in this chapter is to reflect on the immediacy of God as that comes to expression in his being, his knowledge, and his works, including in the latter the works of God internal to the Godhead, the *opera ad intra*, and his works external to the Godhead, the *opera ad extra*.

The question of whether God exists does not detain us at length. To the contrary, we have stated that our basic apologetic presupposition is that *God is*. It might be rejoined that we have thereby denied the significance of rational inquiry even before we have begun the journey into knowledge. We have abolished the possibility of meaning, of rational apprehension, it might be said, before we have even begun to contemplate whether meaning is in fact possible. But we reject forcibly such a counterclaim. For the irony in it is that rational inquiry is possible on our part only because in order to conduct it we stand on the ground that God himself has spoken into existence. The irony of atheism, if it is proposed as a consistent belief system, is that in order to deny the existence of God it is necessary to stand on his property and to look into his face.

The point can be stated differently. There are no atheists. There are not, that is to say, any individuals who know that God does not exist. Further, there are no individuals who are consistently agnostic on the question, in that they hold to the conclusion that God might or might not exist. The philosopher, Immanuel Kant, writing at the culmination of the eighteenth-century Enlightenment, argued against the logical validity of what had to that time been elaborated as so-called proofs of the existence of God. But when he confined God to what he referred to as the noumenal realm and claimed that it was not possible to have any knowledge of things in that realm (he confined the possibility of knowledge to the phenomenal realm), he admitted that just as it was impossible to prove that God existed, so it was impossible to prove that he did not exist. It is quite true that confident claims of agnosticism of that order can be, and have been, made. The claim to agnosticism may appear to have been well established. But because it is true that all men, all instances of human consciousness, are in the hands of God, God can, and as history demonstrates he undoubtedly does, leave individuals to the hardened result of their suppression of the knowledge of him (Rom 1:18).

Consider, on the contrary, our first parent, Adam, who was created as the image of God. For Adam, to be was to know. He knew that he had come from the hands of his Creator. He enjoyed the privilege of walking with God in the preincarnate appearance of the Second Person of the Godhead "in the garden in the cool of the day" (Gen 3:8). And so the sense of God, the *sensus deitatis*, along with the seed of religion and the conviction of the necessity of worshiping God, the *semen religionis*, is innate in the human consciousness. Every man knows that God is, and that he is therefore without excuse in the presence of God. In the very act of self-awareness man is aware of God. Or at least that awareness and the consciousness of the obligation it carries with it have existed until, conceivably, God has withdrawn his overtures. "[T]hat which may be known of God is manifest in them. . . . For the invisible things of him from the creation of the world are clearly seen, being understood by the things that are made, even his eternal power and Godhead; so that they are without excuse" (Rom 1:19-20). But it is equally true that by their rejection and suppression of the awakening awareness of God it may follow for some that "God gave them up" (Rom 1:24). That is the potential outcome of the pretense of atheism. What we are saying is that there are no *psychological* atheists. There may be, and there undoubtedly are, *practical* atheists, people who live and think as though there is no God. But every person knows that God is.

The awareness of God is inescapable and deeply embedded in the human consciousness. The fact that absolute being, absolute personhood, and absolute meaning and knowledge exist in God establishes meaning in the external reality that he spoke into existence. That follows from the fact, as we have already observed, that we are the analogue of God both as to our being and our knowledge. It is consistent with that to say that our presuppositional argument is sustained by reason that we hold to the impossibility of the contrary, meaning that any contrary assumption implies that the universe is a universe of randomness and chance, without a principle of coherence, without meaning, and without possibility of explanation. There are, of course, claims contrary to our presupposition, even within the apologetic literature of the church. John Blanchard, for example, in a purportedly Christian apologetic that runs counter to our presupposition, capitulates entirely to rationalism in his argument that "the right approach to the subject of the existence of God is to assemble and assess all of the data we can and then come to a conclusion based on what we consider satisfying evidence or reasonable probabilities."[1] We reject Blanchard's alignment with Alister McGrath in the claim that "The attempt to establish primary truths on which we can build absolute knowledge has proved to be futile . . . All our knowledge about anything that really matters is a matter of probability."[2] As to the logical consistency of the concept of probability, it can be said that only that is possible, or "probable," which God has already ordained.

Foremost among the so-called proofs of the existence of God is what has been referred to as the ontological proof. It has enjoyed a wide currency since Anselm's (1033–1109) first statement of it. It continues to be a matter of lively dispute in the philosophic literature. The essence of Anselm's statement is that it is possible to conceive of a being "than which no greater can be thought," and, further, that the being which is so conceived must necessarily exist in reality.[3] Anselm's argument claims that "Therefore, if that than which nothing greater can be conceived exists *in the understanding alone*, the very being than which nothing greater can be conceived is one than which a greater *can* be conceived. But obviously this is impossible. Hence there is no doubt that there exists a being than which nothing greater can be conceived, and it exists *both in understanding and reality*."[4] The problem with Anselm's proof, as Gaunilo, an opponent of Anselm, argued at the time, is that it was not possible as Anselm had claimed to argue from the subjective conception of such a being as was contemplated to his, or its, objective existence in reality. The real existence

---

1. Blanchard, *Does God believe in atheists?*, 194.

2. Idem. See also for a strong dissent from our presuppositional apologetic Sproul et al., *Classical Apologetics*.

3. The argument was set forth in Anselm's *Monologium* or *Soliloquy* and later stated in more complete form in his *Proslogium*. The "proof" is discussed in Schaff, *History of the Christian Church*, vol. 5, 601f., and, for a modern view, in Reymond, *New Systematic Theology*, 132f.

4. Cited in Reymond, op. cit., 132, italics added.

of a thing must first be established, Gaunilo argued, before anything can be predicated of it.

The ontological proof was again formulated by Descartes at the beginning of modern philosophy in the seventeenth century,[5] and in due course it attracted, most notably at the hands of Kant, the same objections as Gaunilo had stated.[6] It is generally agreed that Anselm's argument fails by reason that existence cannot be taken to be a predicate in the sense intended. A contemporary apologist, R. C. Sproul, has claimed to have remedied Anselm's logically defective argument as follows: "When one adds the simple observation that the necessary proof of anything is the inability to think of its nonexistence, this establishes the necessary existence of the perfect being.... When one adds that Anselm's being, than which none greater can be conceived, cannot be thought to not exist, he has proven the actual necessary real existence of that being."[7] A response to Sproul is that he does not present at that point any grounds to justify his claim that it is not possible to think the nonexistence of God. If the thought of nonexistence is impossible, as we have argued as the basis of our presupposition, a claim to that effect must rest on the *sensus deitatis* that is created, and therefore inescapable, within the human consciousness. But Sproul presents his "rational defense of the Christian faith," as he refers to it, as a forthright rebuttal of presuppositional apologetics, and his evidential apologetic embraces an underlying rationalism. He thereby rejects at that point the only ground that might sustain his argument. As to the impossibility of the thought of nonexistence, however, Sproul follows Jonathan Edwards who states that we have an idea of being and cannot have an idea of nonbeing. "That there should be nothing at all is utterly impossible."[8] Other theologians, apart from contemporary philosophers including, notably, Kurt Gödel, Charles Hartshorne, Norman Malcolm, and Alvin Plantinga, have discussed the ontological proof that need not detain us at further length.[9]

---

5. Descartes, *Discourse on Method*. The ontological proof argument, grounded for Descartes in his "idea of a perfect Being," appears in Part IV of the *Discourse*.

6. See Kant, *Critique of Pure Reason*, 410–18. Cited in Sproul, op. cit., 31.

7. Sproul et al., op. cit., 103–4.

8. Edwards, *Freedom of the Will*, 186, cited in Sproul et al., op. cit., 106.

9. Among Reformed theologians Shedd attempts a defense of Anselm in his *Dogmatic Theology*, vol. 1, 224. For modern treatments see Plantinga, ed., *The Ontological Argument*. Note in Plantinga, op. cit., 155–56, Norman Malcolm, "Malcolm's Statement of Anselm's

We have noted this argument and attempts at a proof of the existence of God (leaving aside other so-called proofs) for several reasons. First, it does itself contain, or is grounded in, a significant truth. That is that the sensibility of the being and the existence of God does exist as an ineradicable intuition in the human mind. As has been said, there exists in the human consciousness an ineradicable, if nevertheless suppressed, *sensus deitatis*, the sense of God. The Psalmist cautions us, "The fool hath said in his heart, There is no God" (Ps 14:1). Second, the construction of arguments of the kind reviewed nevertheless serves as an instance of the assumed competence of the human mind, an incipient rationalism of the kind that we set out to avoid in our apologetic postulate of presupposition. The argument of the "proofs" is an argument from man to God. That is instanced, for example, in Descartes, whose form of the ontological proof in his *Discourse on Reason* is grounded in his "idea of a Perfect Being."[10] But the starting point of Descartes' system, and his dictum that "we ought never to allow ourselves to be persuaded of the truth of anything unless on the evidence of our reason,"[11] involved the assumption of the hegemony of reason and places Descartes at the beginning of a new rationalism.

TRIUNE GOD

That God exists in three Persons is not a truth discoverable by autonomous human reason. It is part of the "mystery of godliness" (1 Tim 3:16). But the reality of the Trinity of the Godhead is clearly revealed in the pages of Scripture. We do not pause to rehearse the Scriptural documentation at length. The divinity of the man Jesus Christ is well displayed in the text. Suffice it to say that "In the beginning was the Word, and the Word was with God, and the Word was God" (John 1:1); "[W]hen the fulness of the time was come, God sent forth his Son, made of a woman, made under the law, to redeem them that were under the law" (Gal 4:4–5); "God . . . loved us, and sent his Son to be the propitiation for our sins" (1 John 4:10); "I and my Father are one" (John 10:30). And the divine personality of the Holy Spirit is similarly established extensively in the Scriptures. In the course of the supper discourses on the night on which he was betrayed Christ said to the disciples that "It is expedient for you that I go away; for

---

Ontological Argument," cited in Sproul et al., op. cit., 105.

10. See footnote 5.

11. See the concluding paragraph of Part IV of the *Discourse on Method*.

if I go not away, the Comforter will not come unto you; but if I depart, I will send him unto you.... [and] when he, the Spirit of truth, is come, he will guide you into all truth" (John 16:7, 13). We note the personal pronouns "him" and "he" in Christ's reference to his sending the Holy Spirit. It is clear that the promise of Christ was fulfilled on the day of Pentecost, when the Spirit of God came upon the church in a new fullness, thereby fulfilling the prophecy of Joel (Acts 2:16; Joel 2:28–32). The Scriptural data are copious.

But the immediacy of God as to his being, his aseity or, as Bavinck stated it, the fact that "Whatever God is he is of himself," implies also the autotheotic nature of God the Son and God the Holy Spirit. When it is said that the essence of the Godhead resides in the Second and the Third Persons of the divine Trinity, it is not being said that the essence of God is in some respect shared or distributed among them. For the full essence of God dwells fully in each of the Persons. The Father, the Son, and the Holy Spirit are each fully God. It is accordingly necessary to raise a question that has troubled the church, particularly in the early formation of its confessional theology, regarding the subordination or otherwise that exists among and between the divine Persons. Suffice it to say at this point that the mystery of the triune existence of God requires it to be said that the divine mind and the divine will are fully in each of the Persons. All of the divine attributes in which the essence of God is expressed, the incommunicable attributes of infinity, eternity, and immutability, for example, reside fully in each of the Persons. We refer, therefore, to the consubstantiality of the Persons of the Godhead. The Westminster Shorter Catechism (1647) states that "There are three persons in the Godhead: the Father, the Son, and the Holy Ghost; and these three are one God, *the same in substance*, equal in power and glory."[12] We shall return to those doctrinally critical issues.

Before we look further at the being and actions of God, however, it is necessary to bring into focus again the unique identity of the Son, the Second Person of the Trinity who came into this world as man for our redemption. We have already observed that Jesus Christ, fully man and fully God, was not a human person. He was not a divine-human person. He was a divine Person who assumed into union with his divine nature a

---

12. Westminster Shorter Catechism, Question 6, italics added.

human nature, a "true body and a reasonable soul,"[13] yet without sin. In his incarnation Christ, "being in the form of God" (Phil 2:6) or, that is, fully God, "the brightness of his glory, and the express image of his person" (Heb 1:3), did not in any sense lay aside or divest himself of his divine identity and glory. He did, in order to discharge his messianic-redemptive assignment in this world, lay aside the *insignia* or the *signs* of his glory. But as to his divine nature there resided in him, as has just been said, the full essence of the Godhead. The apostle John has stated that clearly in his reference to Christ as "the Son of man which is in heaven" (John 3:13). When our Lord was in this world he was, as to his divine nature, both in this world and in heaven, while as to his human nature he was in the world.[14] It follows that now, in his eternal session at the right hand of the Father, Christ is in his human nature in heaven, while in his divine nature he is both in heaven and in the world.

It became necessary in the early history of the church to defend strenuously the doctrine of the divine personhood of Christ. He has been called the theanthropic person, combining the Greek words θέος [theos] meaning God and ἄνθρωπος [anthropos] meaning man. The designation is appropriate, provided it is understood to imply the distinctions that orthodox theology has found it necessary to make. Shedd, for example, concludes on the point that "The Trinitarian personality of the Son of God did not begin at the incarnation, but the *theanthropic* personality of Jesus Christ did. It is the divine nature, and not the human, which is the base of Christ's person."[15] And further, "[T]he divine nature constantly supports the human nature under all the temptations to sin that are presented to it . . . . [but] It deserts the humanity so that it may suffer for the *atonement of sin*, but it never deserts the humanity so that it may *fall into sin itself.*"[16]

---

13. Westminster Shorter Catechism, Question 22.

14. The text referred to, John 3:13, appears as stated in the *Textus Receptus* but the words "which is in heaven" have been omitted from the modern texts such as the twenty-sixth edition of the Nestle-Aland Greek New Testament and the United Bible Societies third edition. A critical discussion and support for the inclusion of the phrase and the doctrine implicit in it is contained in Hendriksen, *New Testament Commentary: John*, vol. 2, 500–1.

15. Shedd, op. cit., vol. 2, 269.

16. Ibid., 335, italics added.

The biblical doctrine of the Person of Christ was brought to clear formulation in the early church, following certain heresies that had developed in relation to it. That doctrine quickly came under attack even in the apostolic times. In his letter to the Colossian church Paul found it necessary to refute certain heresies that were akin to what later became a more fully developed Gnosticism, and John in his first epistle was very much concerned with the same problem. Gnosticism in its many expressions and aspects was essentially a heresy that denied the reality of the deity and divinity of Christ. It argued, for example, that there could not have been a true union of spirit with matter. Divinity, in which essential goodness inhered, could not come into union with humanity and matter in which, it was supposed, evil inhered. It was impossible, therefore, it was claimed, that Jesus Christ could be both divine and human. One expression of Gnosticism (Docetism) argued that Jesus Christ was a man on whom and to whom the Spirit of God came at an early stage of his life, but that the Spirit departed from him before his death.[17]

In the post-apostolic age similar problems arose. The followers of Sabellius, a presbyter of Ptolemais in the years 250–260, admitted that a distinction within the Godhead is set forth in Scripture, but the Sabellian system of thought denied that the distinction was a personal one. It asserted "that the Father, the Son, and the Holy Spirit are just three different names for one and the same person, viewed under different aspects or relations."[18] The distinction within the Godhead, the Sabellians claimed, was "merely nominal or modal."[19] Put differently, Sabellius understood by "the Logos [the Son] and the Holy Spirit two Powers (δυνάμεις) [dynameis] streaming forth from the divine Essence, through which God works and reveals himself."[20] While Sabellianism did not become an accepted part of the dogma of the church and was held by only certain individuals, the worthy Athanasius in the fourth century rejected it and also the Arian doctrine forcibly. Shedd sums up his critique by saying that "He [Athanasius] describes the Sabellian Trinitarian process as a 'dilatation and contraction,' an 'expanding and collapsing' of the Divine Essence."[21]

---

17. On Docetism and Gnosticism see Cunningham, *Historical Theology*, vol. 1, 124–25; Hägglund, *History of Theology*, 21.

18. Cunningham, op. cit., vol. 1, 272.

19. Idem.

20. Shedd, *History of Christian Doctrine*, vol. 1, 257.

21. See ibid., 260–61n.

Athanasius also stood strenuously against the virulent heresy that had been promulgated by Arius, a presbyter of Alexandria in the early fourth century, and that had been condemned by the Synod of Alexandria in 321. It was addressed and condemned again at the Council of Nicea in the year 325. At issue again was the doctrine of the consubstantiality of the Son with the Father. The Nicene Creed asserted that "the Son was ὁμοούσιος [homoousios] of the same substance with the Father, but also, moreover, that He was begotten of the substance of the Father, and, of course, had a substance not only of the same in kind, but numerically one with His."[22] The "homoousios" doctrine had been earlier deduced and stated by Alexander, bishop of Alexandria, in opposition to Arius. Against the Arian heresy, the doctrine was thereby stated that while there exists three Persons within the Godhead and each Person is characterized by distinguishable properties, it is to be said and maintained that the divine nature, the divine essence, exists fully in each of the Persons. In that manner, Nicea insisted on the autotheotic nature of the Son of God.[23]

The Arians dissented from that well-formulated doctrine. For them, the Son was not "homoousios," but "homoiousios." Note that the insertion of the "i" (the Greek iota, ι) changes the meaning of the statement from "of one substance with the Father" to that of being "like the Father." The import of the Arian claim was that the Son did not participate in the primary essence of the Father. The Son, Arius claimed, was "not divine in *any* sense, but is strictly a creature, though the very highest and first of all."[24]

The autotheotic nature of Christ, which will engage us again below when the works of God internal to the Godhead are brought briefly in review, was thus clearly stated at Nicea in 325 and it was confirmed by the Council of Constantinople in 381. It was settled in creedal form by the Council of Chalcedon in the year 451. The Christological settlement of Chalcedon stated that the divine and human natures were joined in union in Christ, without confusion, without change, without division, and without separation. The first two of those defining characteristics insist

---

22. Cunningham, *Historical Theology*, vol. 1, 284.

23. Turretin (1623–87), a successor of John Calvin in Geneva, discusses the relevant doctrines and observes that "Although there are more persons than one in God, yet there are not more natures. All persons partake of one and the same infinite nature, not by division, but by communication." Turretin, *Institutes*, vol. 1, 182.

24. Shedd, *History*, vol. 1, 307. See Shedd's extended discussion of the early Christological controversies in ibid., 246ff., on "Ante-Nicene Trinitarianism."

on the fact that there was no communication of properties between the divine and the human natures. At the incarnation, when Christ took to himself the created human nature that had been prepared for him, there was no commingling of the eternal and the temporal. The second two of the terms describing the Person of Christ insist on and guard the reality of the union.

THE ASEITY AND TIMELESSNESS OF GOD

We have spoken of God's aseity, or of his independence and self-existence and his timeless existence in eternity. God is not dependent for his existence on any cause external to himself. He is self-caused. John Frame states that when that latter term is used with reference to God it means that "God is uncaused and has within himself sufficient reasons or grounds for his existence."[25] Bavinck, whose conclusions regarding God's existence we referred to previously, had stated that God is "the completely independent, only, *absolute* Being ... who has the ground of his existence in himself."[26] God's "aseity (absolute essence) may be called the primary attribute of God's being."[27] Frame observes that Van Til, following in the same tradition as Bavinck, "refer(s) to God as self-contained, meaning 'that God is in no sense correlative to or dependent upon anything besides his own being.'"[28] Van Til has further referred to the existence of God in the following terms: "God may be said to be *causa sui*, if by *causa sui* is meant the reason for and meaning of his existence. He is self-contained rationality. His rationality is not something he possesses, but is something with which his being is coterminous."[29]

But differences of view have arisen regarding God's timeless existence in eternity. We noted in the preceding chapter Helm's dissent from certain modern philosophies on the matter of God's timelessness and his rejection of certain implications of process theology.[30] Augustine had tried to unravel the meaning of time in the eleventh chapter of his *Confessions* on "Time and Eternity." "It is not in time that you precede times," Augustine

---

25. Frame, *Doctrine of God*, 601.
26. Bavinck, *Doctrine of God*, 126.
27. Ibid., 127.
28. Van Til, *Defense of the Faith*, 9. Cited in Frame, *Doctrine of God*, 601n.
29. Van Til, *Systematic Theology*, 206.
30. See chapter 1, n.12, 13.

states in his address to God. "Otherwise you would not precede all times. In the sublimity of an eternity which is always in the present, you are before all things past and transcend all things future . . . 'But you are the same and your years do not fail' (Ps 102:27). Your 'years' neither go nor come. . . . Your 'years' are 'one day' (Ps 90:4; 2 Pet 3:8), and your 'day' is not any and every day but Today. . . Your Today is eternity. So you begat one coeternal with you, to whom you said: 'Today I have begotten you'. . . . There was therefore no time when you had not made something, because you made time itself."[31]

But the notion of God's timelessness has also been the subject of debate. It has not attracted the concurrence of all contemporary theologians. Robert Reymond, for example, has surveyed Scriptural texts that "clearly ascribe everlastingness to God," but he argues that "what is not so clear is whether his everlasting existence should be understood, with most classical Christian thinkers (for example, Augustine, Anselm, Aquinas), as also involving the notion of *timelessness*."[32] Reymond is worried that it seems to him to be "sheer dogmatism to declare, because God is omniscient . . . that there can be no consciousness of successive duration in his mind."[33] Recalling the comment of Helm on historic theological attitudes to this question,[34] Reymond suggests that "it is a *non sequitur* to conclude from the fact of God's omniscience that God has no *idea of succession*, that is, that relative to his own existence he has no knowledge of a past, present, and future applicable to his own existence."[35] At that point Reymond relies on Dabney, a prominent theologian and philosopher in nineteenth-century America,[36] but in doing so he fails to acknowledge Dabney's distinction between God's "existence without succession . . . existence not related to time" and the "consciousness of his own subsistence."[37] Dabney wisely concludes, however, that argument in this area is in danger of producing "one of those 'antinomies' which emerge, when we strive to comprehend the incomprehensible."[38]

31. Augustine, *Confessions*, 230.
32. Reymond, *New Systematic Theology*, 172.
33. Ibid., 173.
34. See chapter 1, n. 12, 13.
35. Reymond, op. cit., 173.
36. See Dabney, *Lectures in Systematic Theology*.
37. See Dabney, op. cit., 39–40.
38. Ibid., 40.

But it is worth considering in these respects that as Reymond suggests, a distinction might be contemplated between the ontological and the epistemological. "This would mean that, for God, while he himself ever remains *ontologically* unaffected by durational sequence (that is, his consciousness of his sequential duration in no way impinges negatively upon his 'Godness') and while his thoughts themselves (that is, his wisdom and knowledge) are eternally intuited, comprehensive, and teleologically ordered and *not* arrived at chronologically through the discursive process, nevertheless, the concept or idea of the possibility of 'before' and 'after' in durational sequence or succession is a distinct *epistemological* category applicable to him as to us."[39] But again, such an ontological-epistemological distinction has in no sense drawn widespread assent.

Van Til has addressed this same nexus of ideas and observed that "if we introduce time or succession of moments into the *consciousness* of God in order that we may understand how God is related to time we have to ask ourselves in turn how the consciousness of God is related to the *being* of God. Thus we should have to introduce succession of moments into the being of God for the same reason that we have introduced it into the consciousness of God."[40] While wisdom dictates that we avoid at this point Dabney's "antinomies," it would seem appropriate to say that there is no succession of moments in the knowledge of God or the being of God. While he has knowledge of sequences of time events, he does not know those sequences sequentially. He therefore has no memory of what has been, in the sense of his having become aware of it, or expectation of his own future that he must wait to discover. Perhaps the issues are best resolved in the manner in which Dabney states it: "[S]ince all God's knowledge is absolutely true to the actual realities known, wherever he knows one thing as destined to depend on another thing, there must be a case in which God *thinks a sequence.* Let the distinction be clearly grasped. The things are known to God as in sequence; but his own subjective act of thought concerning them is not a sequence.... while the infinite capacity of the divine mind enables it to see coëtaneously by one all-including intuition every particular truth of his omniscience, his absolute infallibility also insures the mental arrangement of them all in their logical and

---

39. Reymond, op. cit., 176–77.
40. Van Til, *Defense of the Faith*, 36, italics added.

causal relations, as they are destined to be actualized in successive time."[41] Jonathan Edwards has commented that "There is no succession in God's knowledge."[42]

But against those well-discussed aspects of God's knowledge, a further significant question has arisen historically. What is to be said of God's so-called "middle knowledge," sometimes referred to as molinism after the Jesuit L. Molina (1536–1600), and of the implications it has for God's relations with the world? By that we refer to knowledge that is "middle" in the sense that it is "between God's *necessary knowledge* of himself and all possible things because he is *necessarily* omniscient and his 'free knowledge' of all actual things, past, present, and future, because he *freely* willed these things."[43] A distinction is conjured, that is, between God's knowledge of what could, or might, possibly occur in reality and what he has in fact ordained to come to pass. God may, so it might be thought, know what men will freely choose to do without his having specifically decreed their actions. Certain modern theologies, Arminianism, Open Theism, and the earlier Socinianism, have based their conclusions on just such a supposition. They have made use of it to explain the matter of man's salvation. William Craig has commented in this connection that "[God] knows what any free creature would do in any situation [and thus] can, by creating the appropriate situations, bring it about that creatures will achieve his ends and purposes and . . . will do so freely."[44] But if human actions were reckoned to be indeterminate, or absolutely arbitrary or contingent, it is difficult to conclude that they could be known even if divinely created conditions were extant as has just been supposed. For the assumption of absolute indeterminacy of human action would imply that they were *not* determined by the postulated divine arrangements. It would seem, then, that, as Reymond concluded, "human indeterminism excludes divine middle knowledge."[45]

That leaves open, however, the relation of Arminianism and the Open theism theology to the knowledge of God. A difference is in view at that point. Arminianism makes use of the molinist conclusions to state

41. Dabney, *Discussions*, vol. 1, 294.
42. Jonathan Edwards, *Freedom of the Will*, Morgan, PA edition, 144.
43. Reymond, op. cit., 189n.
44. Craig, *The Only Wise God*, 135, cited in Reymond, op. cit., 189.
45. Reymond, op. cit., 189. Note Reymond's reference to Frame's critique of Helm's *Providence of God*.

that God does, by virtue of his omniscience, have knowledge of what the actions of men will be under circumstances that he brings to pass. Specifically, God knows which individuals will respond to the call of his gospel and will, by the exercise of their free wills, express repentance and faith in Christ. Those individuals, then, by reason of God's foreknowledge based on those postulates, are the ones whom God has decreed and predestined to be saved. By that means, moreover, the mystery of God's predestination is resolved. But it is resolved, it is not difficult to see, by the importation of the assumption of the sovereignty of the human volitional capacity. All that has been said of the immediacy of God and of his covenantal purpose is thereby denied. The resolution that Arminianism purports to provide is then sub-biblical.

The Open Theism theology of recent vintage takes a significant step beyond classic Arminianism. In the latter scheme, God is reckoned to know the future actions of men for the reasons and on the grounds that have been stated. In the former, to the contrary, God is assumed *not* to know what the future actions and decisions of men will be, and the future is assumed to be, for God, completely open. That is the point at which the Open Theism holds the same notions of the changeability of God as we observed in the process theology. The assumption of the ignorance of God as to future events runs counter to, as appears quite clearly on the surface, and it destroys, what we have acknowledged to this point to be the omniscience of God. The Open Theism rejoinder is to the effect that God is indeed omniscient, but by that it is meant that he is omniscient in the sense that he fully knows all there is to be known. But the future, being open, is not yet available to be known. Therefore, of course, God does not know it.[46]

When it has been said, as we have observed, that God knows all things in one eternal act of knowing, we are alerted to the difference between the what and the how of man's knowledge on the one hand, and that of God's

---

46. On the theology of Open Theism see, in addition to Frame and Wright as cited, Strimple, "What does God Know?" in John H. Armstrong, ed., *The Coming Evangelical Crisis*, 140–41, cited in Frame, *No Other God*, 34. On the earlier Socinianism, Cunningham comments that the Socinians "admit indeed that God knows all things that are knowable; but then they contend that future contingent events, such as the future actions of responsible agents, are *not* knowable—do not come within the scope of what may be known, even by an infinite Being; and, upon this ground, they allege that it is no derogation from the omniscience of God, that He does not, and cannot, know what is not knowable." *Historical Theology*, vol. 2, 173.

knowledge on the other. Christian philosophers have discussed whether the difference is essentially qualitative or merely quantitative. The *manner* of God's knowing is clearly different. But it follows also from what has been said that the difference is qualitative because the meaning of facts (we have previously said that all the facts are God's facts), and the meaning of all of the constellations of facts and the structural relations between them, are fully defined in the mind of God but are less than comprehensively conceivable for man. Man's knowledge is knowledge within, and is structured by, a temporal process. God's knowledge, on the other hand, is, for all the reasons we have seen, not temporal at all. God does not know as the result of a process of investigation. He does not, and could not, wait to discover. He does not hold, therefore, any expectation as to what might or might not eventuate. Man knows sequentially. His epistemic capacity, or what he knows as well as what is available to be known, is different on, say, Thursday from what it had been on the preceding Monday. For Thursday has a different history from Monday. It holds within it different possibilities and potentialities of subsequent events and therefore of the knowledge of them. God, we have said, knows sequences, but he does not know them sequentially. That is because he ordered them and ordained them and structured their processes and outcomes. We may put the point differently. There does not exist any "possibility," as a category determinative of action, beyond God. God has not confronted and considered the possibility of eventuation that he has not ordained. Or from our point of view, possibility exists for man, but only that is possible which God has ordained.

The relation between the knowledge that God possesses and our knowledge can be stated by saying that our finite knowledge is an analogue of God's infinite knowledge. To say that our knowledge is analogical is in no sense to say that it is not real or true knowledge. Our knowledge of God in his being is an analogue of God's knowledge of himself. In one respect we have no access to knowledge of the essence of God. But to the extent that his essence is displayed in his attributes which he has revealed in his self-disclosure, we know him as he is. Our knowledge of the world, of its structure and its history, is again an analogue of God's knowledge. In every case the knowledge is true because God has established an accordance or correspondence between the facts in their comprehensive reality as he has established and sees them and our finite apprehension of them. Put in another way, as Van Til has argued, "[W]hen we think of human knowledge, correspondence is of primary importance. If there is to be true coherence in our knowledge there must be correspondence between our idea of facts and God's ideas of these facts. Or rather we should say that our ideas must correspond to God's ideas."[47] God establishes that correspondence, in that our knowledge is a finite replica of his knowledge. Our knowledge on every level on which knowledge is available to us is accordingly true, though in the nature of the case it is not, and cannot be, comprehensive knowledge.

THE WORKS OF GOD

What we have referred to as *the immediacy of God* has been elaborated in the foregoing with reference to God's being, his eternity, his aseity, his independence outside of time, and the knowledge that he therein possesses. In that, God is transcendent beyond all that he has made. Yet theologians have spoken extensively of God's immanence, meaning by that his presence in the course of human history and his providential ordering of it by his Spirit. The relations involved acquire focus from a consideration of the works of God, meaning by that both his works *ad intra* and his works *ad extra*. By those categories we mean, respectively, the works of God *internal* to the Godhead, and his works *external* to the Godhead.

The *opera ad intra* can be referred to briefly as taking up God's threefold actions outside of time in, first, the eternal generation of the Son; second, the spiration or the breathing forth of the Spirit; and third, the decrees of God that set forth his covenantal purpose in relation to the reality, including mankind created in his image, that he had established. The *opera ad intra* communicate, further, the meaning of the autotheotic natures of God the Son and God the Holy Spirit. Of God the Son, for example, we say that as to his nature he is autotheotic, while as to his Person he is of the Father. Calvin has argued to similar effect. "Therefore we say that deity in an absolute sense exists of itself; whence likewise we confess that the Son since he is God, exists of himself, but not in respect of his Person; indeed, since he is the Son, we say that he exists from the Father. Thus his *essence* is without beginning; while the beginning of his *person* is God himself."[48] The mystery of the *opera ad intra* is that in the eternal generation, the eternal begetting, of the Son, the Father did not, in

---

47. See the discussion in Bahnsen, *Van Til's Apologetics*, 169.
48. Calvin, *Institutes*, vol. 1, 154, italics added.

a manner inscrutable to us, *create* the Son and communicate his essence to him, but that he established the Son *within* the divine essence.

Berkhof has made the same point. It would be incorrect to imagine, he says, "that the Father first generated a second person, and then communicated the divine essence to that person, for that would lead to the conclusion that the Son was not generated out of the divine essence, but was created out of nothing."[49] Berkhof concludes properly on the generation of the Son that "*It is that eternal and necessary act of the first person in the Trinity, whereby He, within the divine Being, is the ground of a second personal subsistence like His own, and puts the second person in possession of the whole divine essence, without any division, alienation, or change*."[50]

When we say that God the Son is begotten of the Father, it follows that the distinguishing and personal property of the Father is that he is not begotten, or, in other words, that he is unbegotten in himself. It can be said that the work of the Father that is strictly attributable to him *ad intra* is that of the eternal generation of the Son. For the spiration or the breathing forth of the Holy Spirit is the work jointly of the Father and the Son. We shall return to the point. But the mystery of the works of God *ad intra* are necessarily, by reason of our createdness and finitude, not available to our comprehension. The veil of mystery has not been, and cannot be, withdrawn. Cunningham's comment is judicious when he refers to "the communication from eternity *in some mysterious and ineffable way* of the divine nature and substance by the Father to the Son."[51] When we hold to the eternal autotheotic nature of the Son with the Father and at the same time maintain his personal eternal subsistence, we reject the claims of the Sabellians and the modalists who argue that the Son is simply and only a mode of expression or manifestation of, or emanation from, the Father who is the one eternal God.

As to his distinguishing and personal property, the Son shares with the Father in the spiration of the Spirit. When the early church considered the relation of the Holy Spirit to the First and Second Persons of the Trinity it was clearly held that the Spirit, as well as the Son, is of the same essence as the Father and that he and the Father, with the Son, are therefore consubstantial. In the same way as we have said that the Son as to his nature is

---

49. Berkhof, *Systematic Theology*, 94.
50. Idem.
51. Cunningham, *Historical Theology*, vol. 1, 296, italics added.

autotheotic but as to his Person he is of the Father, we say also that the Holy Spirit as to his nature is autotheotic but as to his Person he is of the Father and the Son. A difference of view arose historically, however, as to whether the Spirit proceeded only and uniquely from the Father or from the Father and the Son together. The Nicene Creed as we have it at the present time states that "we believe in the Holy Spirit . . . who proceeds *from the Father and the Son.*"[52] The matter was settled in creedal form at the Synod of Toledo in 589 when the word *filioque* (which means "and from the Son") was added to the previously existing Niceno-Constantinopolitan creed. While the word *filioque* had been in currency at the time of the earlier councils of the church, it was incorporated in the creed in the form in which we now possess it only at the later time. Its incorporation in the creed gave rise to what was henceforth referred to as "the Filioque clause," and its adoption became the occasion of a divergence between the Western and Eastern churches that remains current at the present time.[53] The Eastern church continues to reject the filioque clause.

Berkhof again summarizes the relevant issue by defining the *spiration* involved as *"that eternal and necessary act of the first and second persons in the Trinity whereby they, within the divine Being, become the ground of the personal subsistence of the Holy Spirit, and put the third person in possession of the whole divine essence, without any division, alienation, or change."*[54]

A final question that has caused some difficulty in the history of the church warrants a brief notice. Given the doctrine of *theology* as we have elaborated it, that is the doctrine of God in his eternal being, is it to be understood that any subordination exists between the divine Persons? Our answer turns on the contemplation of the divine Trinity under the heads of what has been properly referred to as the *ontological trinity* on the one hand, and the *economic trinity* on the other. Or more precisely, we may contemplate the Trinity in, respectively, its *ontological* aspect and in its *economic* aspect. The ontological aspect refers to God in his being, as that has been the subject of our discussion to this point. In that aspect, and holding to the consubstantiality of the divine Persons in the divine essence, there is no subordination within the Godhead. Each of the persons is fully God. The economic aspect, on the other hand, refers to the

---

52. The Nicene Creed, various editions. See *Trinity Hymnal*, 846.

53. See Noll, *Turning Points*, 129ff. for a valuable discussion of the "Division between East and West: The Great Schism (1054)" and the *filioque* dispute and controversy.

54. Berkhof, op. cit., 97.

actions of the distinguishable Persons of the Godhead in the effectuation of the acts of God external to the Godhead, or in, that is, the *opera ad extra*. In particular, when reference is made to the eternal formulation of God's covenant of redemption it will be seen that distinguishable redemptive offices were assumed by the respective Persons of the Godhead. To anticipate briefly at this point, it was determined in the eternal council of the Godhead that the office of the Father was to elect a designated people as the subjects of his decree to redeem. It was the redemptive office of the Son to undertake the redemptive assignment that necessitated his incarnation in this world and his life of obedience and his death on behalf of those subjects. It was correspondingly the undertaken and committed redemptive office of the Holy Spirit to apply to those people for whom Christ died the benefits of his redemption, the gifts that he purchased for them, notably the gifts of repentance, faith, and righteousness, and to conduct them to glory.

In the execution of the redemptive offices, then, there was and is of necessity a subordination between the divine Persons. But the subordination that exists is an *official* subordination, having to do with office, and not an *essential* subordination. When we say that there was no subordination within the ontological trinity but that a subordination existed within the economic trinity in the realization of the Persons' respective redemptive offices, we can say the following without damage to that conclusion. As Charles Hodge, the nineteenth-century Princeton theologian, observes, "The Scriptures speak of a threefold subordination of Christ. 1. A subordination as to the *mode* of subsistence and operation, of the second, to the first person of the Trinity; which is perfectly consistent with their identity of substance, and equality in power and glory. 2. the voluntary subordination of the Son in his humbling himself to be found in fashion as a man, and becoming obedient unto death, and therefore subject to the limitations and infirmities of our nature. 3. The economical or official subjection of the theanthropos. That is, the subordination of the incarnate Son of God, in the work of redemption and as the head of the church. He that is by nature equal with God becomes, as it were, officially [having to do with office] subject to him."[55]

The second aspect of the works of God, those external to the Godhead, the *opera ad extra*, relate to God's actions in creation, provi-

---

55. Hodge, *Commentary*, 63, italics added.

dence, and redemption. In each of those works the three Persons of the Godhead are jointly and actively engaged. As to the creation, it is said that "God created the heaven and the earth" and that "*God* said, let there be" (Gen 1:1, 3). And then, "the *Spirit* of God moved upon the face of the waters" (Gen 1:2). And again, "Let *us* make man in our image" (Gen 1:26). The apostle John ascribes the creation to God the Son in his statement that "all things were made by him" (John 1:3), while Paul states, in reference to Christ, that "by him were all things created" (Col 1:16). The three Persons of the Godhead are clearly engaged. We have referred to God's work of creation in our statement that he spoke into existence all of reality external to the Godhead.

God's works of providence are summarized in the catechetical statement that they refer to his "most holy, wise, and powerful preserving and governing all his creatures and all their actions."[56] To that effect, the author of the letter to the Hebrews stated that God in Christ "upholds all things by the word of his power" (Heb 1:3). And the Psalmist has made the point: "O Lord, how manifold are thy works! in wisdom hast thou made them all: all the earth is full of thy riches" (Ps 104:24). "His kingdom ruleth over all" (Ps 103:19). In reference to the Spirit of God the Psalmist concludes: "Whither shall I go from thy spirit?" (Ps 139:7). Of God the Son, Paul stated to the Ephesians that it was his wish and prayer "That Christ may dwell in your hearts" (Eph 3:17), reflecting the statement on his own account that "I live; yet not I, but Christ liveth in me" (Gal 2:20). Scope is clearly opened for a more expansive consideration of God's immanent presence and activity in the world and its history, particularly, as will be seen, in the redemption and the preservation of his covenanted people.

God's works of redemption engage the distinctive operations of the Father, the Son, and the Holy Spirit in their redemptive offices. We have the Holy Spirit's attestation to the righteousness of Christ at several times. A case in point is, on the occasion of the baptism of our Lord, "the Spirit of God descending like a dove, and lighting upon him: And lo a voice from heaven, saying, This is my beloved Son, in whom I am well pleased" (Matt 3:16–17). The same testimony of the Spirit is recorded on the occasion of the transfiguration of Christ (Matt 17:5; Luke 9:35). Who is to say that the same declaration of the Spirit might not have been heard at other times

---

56. Westminster Shorter Catechism, Question 11.

during our Lord's sinless years in this world? And it was "through the eternal Spirit" that Christ offered himself without spot to God" (Heb 9:14).

The recognition of these and many such instances regarding the works of God external to the Godhead recalls the fact that "Known unto God are all his works from the beginning of the world" (Acts 15:18), and that it is "in him we live, and move, and have our being" (Acts 17:28). But as it is clear on the basis of Scriptural testimony that all of God's immanent working in the world, all of the operations of his common grace, serves the design of his redemptive grace and the salvation of the church, we shall defer further observations on the *opera ad extra* to our discussion in the following chapters of the relation between God and man in the matter of redemption. It will be seen at that time that the question arises of the extent to which, given the sovereignty of God in his administration of providence and the terms and necessities of redemption, the assumption of human free will has validity.

THE COVENANTAL DECREE

What has just been said alerts us to the third of what were referred to as the *opera ad intra*, the works of God internal to the Godhead.[57] Given the divine works of the generation of the Son and the spiration of the Holy Spirit, and given the consubstantiality of the Persons of the Godhead, what, it can be asked, is to be said of the intracommunication within the Godhead that gave rise to the *opera ad extra* that we have just considered? In particular, what is to be said of the covenantal decree of redemption that issued from the predeterminate council of God?

In the first place, what is to be held regarding *the immediacy of God* comes sharply to focus at this point. That is because whatever has been revealed as the outcome of the deliberations of the Godhead, and whatever, as a result, eventuates in the world, have no cause beyond, or higher than, the will of God. We have recourse to no higher or more ultimate locus of explanation than the divine will. God "worketh all things after the counsel

---

57. An interesting diagrammatic summary of the works of God suggested by G. H. Kersten is contained in Wilhelmus à Brakel, *The Christian's Reasonable Service*, vol. 1, 193. The diagram places under the heading of the "internal" works of God those relating to his being, the distinguishable Persons, and his decrees, and under the "external" works it places those of creation, providence, and redemption. à Brakel, who published his *magnum opus* in 1700, was a significant theologian in the Dutch Second Reformation movement at that time.

of his own will" (Eph 1:11). We have said that if there were any entity or canon or possibility or will external to God upon which the dictates of his will were dependent or to which he was in any sense obliged, the god of whom we would be speaking would be less than the God of the Scriptures. When the apostle James made reference to the fact that "Of his own will begat he [God] us with the word of truth" (Jas 1:18), he was invoking a reality regarding the will of God that the Scriptural data show to have application to all his works.

Clearly, we are addressing in these statements the mystery of God's deliberative determinations. We have said that God exists in a timeless eternity. His knowledge of himself and of reality external to his Godhead, his thoughts, deliberations, and intentions are not sequential. And yet we here adduce the truth that he decreed all things before the foundation of the world in what we now contemplate as a divine deliberative council. We do so on the basis of Scriptural disclosure. We have it stated, for example, that what was done in the crucifixion of Christ was done because Christ was "delivered by the determinate counsel and foreknowledge of God" (Acts 2:23). And again, what was done against Christ was done because Pilate and the Jews "were gathered together, For to do whatsoever thy [God's] hand and thy counsel determined before to be done" (Acts 4:28). But if it is to be said of the eternal God that there is no succession of moments, no sequences of time, in his being or knowledge, how, then, can it be said that it was a deliberative process that culminated in a divine covenant and statement of purpose? Berkhof has observed judiciously on the point: "The word 'counsel,' which is one of the terms by which the decree is designated, suggests careful deliberation and consultation. It may contain a suggestion of an intercommunication between the three persons of the Godhead."[58] Mystery persists. But the seeming discordance between God's timelessness and his deliberative decisions is alleviated by the recognition that in it we have an anthropomorphism, a statement regarding the actions of God in the language and in terms characteristic of men, (note "anthropos," meaning "man"), of the highest order. Indeed, it is to be said that all of God's revelation is anthropomorphic. In his revelation God has accommodated himself to our humanity and, moreover, to our fallenness from which his redemption has rescued us.

---

58. Berkhof, *Systematic Theology*, 103–4.

Our principal concern in the chapters that follow will be with the eternal covenant of redemption. It was in that connection that the distinctive redemptive offices of the Father, the Son, and the Holy Spirit were assumed. Two immediate questions arise. The following brief comments will anticipate further discussion. First, the *parties* to the covenant of redemption were the Persons of the Godhead in their distinctive personal subsistences. Though the divine mind and the divine will exist fully in each of the Persons, a mutual undertaking and commitment ensued from the divine council. Thus the redemption of God's elect was assured. But we are interested also in the *subjects* of the covenant of redemption, and at that point a difference of view has arisen in the literature of the church.

The question does not need to detain us at length, but it has at times figured prominently in historical theology. In technical terms, are we to take a supralapsarian (before the fall) or an infralapsarian (after the fall) view of the subjects of God's decree to redeem? In brief, supralapsarianism sees the subjects of the covenantal decree as creatable persons, in that God's decree to elect is seen as (logically, not temporally) prior to his decree to create. The alternative view, infralapsarianism, sees those subjects as fallen persons, as they existed in fallen state following Adam's dereliction from his covenantal obligations. Discussion of this controversy has faded from the theological literature in recent times, except, perhaps, for the attempt of Robert Reymond to revive it in his recent *A New Systematic Theology of the Christian Faith*. In that work he takes what he sees as a newly-formulated position of supralapsarianism.[59] We make only two comments.

First, the very state of finitude in which we stand and contemplate God's decrees makes it necessary to acknowledge at the outset again that God's knowledge of his own purposes, decrees, and objectives with relation to us is incomprehensible to us. When we say, then, that the ultimate locus of explanation of God's decrees is lost to us in the unfathomable realities of his own will, we are acknowledging that there is, in fact, a supralapsarian element in what is to be conjured in human language as God's decrees. For nothing is traceable for us beyond the recognition of God's free and sovereign will. We are unable to plumb the depths of its being and operation. It is necessary to guard against the notion that reason, even within the soulish capacities of the regenerate person, is capable of investigation into the mysteries of the Godhead beyond what God has been pleased to

---

59. Reymond, *New Systematic Theology*, 488–502.

reveal to us. We are content to conclude that the resolution of the identity and status of those whom God has included as the subjects of his decree to redeem, or the thought of God as he formed his covenantal designs with relation to them, are finally inaccessible to us. The consideration in the next chapter of the status of man in sin after, and as a result of, Adam's fall will point to the fact that it was from among the fallen posterity of Adam that God elected those whom he chose to redeem and gave to his Son for that purpose.

But while we leave the present question as unresolvable in the being and will of God, it is therefore possible and even necessary to see also an infralapsarian element in the covenant of redemption. The people whom Christ redeemed were fallen individuals who otherwise merited the prospect of eternal perdition for their sin.[60] It may not be wide of the mark to say that God's decrees to elect and save are supralapsarian in the divine thought and contemplation and exercise of will, but infralapsarian in their execution and their implementation in actual historic time. If, then, we are supralapsarian and infralapsarian in different degrees and different respects, our intention is only to recognize the mystery of God's purposes and redemptive intentions, at the same time as we recognize that it is for fallen and lost sinners that Christ died, those who, as the confession has stated, are "enabled to believe to the saving of their souls."[61]

The decrees of God are capable of more extended discussion than we have accorded them in the foregoing. The Westminster Shorter Catechism states that "The decrees of God are his eternal purpose, according to the counsel of his will, whereby, for his own glory, he hath foreordained whatsoever comes to pass."[62] The Psalmist has stated that "The counsel of the Lord standeth for ever, the thoughts of his heart to all generations" (Ps 33:11). In final summary it can be said that in his eternal deliberation God brought to effect, first, the covenant of redemption that we have noted, the parties to which were the Persons of the Godhead in their distinctive

---

60. It is of interest that the Westminster Confession, at III:7, distinguishes between God's decree of predestination to life, which included his passing over certain individuals, or his act of preterition, and the decree of reprobation. The decree of preterition, or the eternal action of God whereby he "withholds his mercy" from some, is "according to the unsearchable counsel of his own will." But the fact that they are "ordain[ed] ... to dishonor and wrath," in the decree of reprobation, is "for their sin." In short, preterition is referable to God's will, while reprobation is referable to the sinner's sin.

61. Westminster Confession of Faith, XIV:1.

62. Westminster Shorter Catechism, Question 7.

subsistences, and that he brought to effect also what has been referred to as a covenant of grace. The distinctive feature of that covenant has to do with the designation of the *parties* to it. The covenant of grace can be properly construed as existing between God on the one hand and those whom he chose to redeem on the other. Or more particularly, it can be stated as bringing to effect the covenant between God and his people as represented by Christ. But with it all, the divine objective of the salvation of God's elect was assured.

We turn in the following chapter to consider the way in which, given what we have seen as *the immediacy of God* in his being and in the design of his purposes, significant aspects of immediacy attach also to the entailment of sin that made redemption necessary and to the *modus operandi*, by the works of the Son and the Holy Spirit, by which that redemption is accomplished and applied to the beneficiaries of it.

3

The Immediate Imputation of Sin

WE BEGIN IN THIS chapter to consider the immediacy of the works of God external to the Godhead, particularly as that applies to the accomplishment of redemption that is contemplated in the covenant of grace. Again we are interested in the question whether any mediacy, or any mediating or secondary cause, exists between certain of the actions and operations of God and the resulting effects in human nature and the human condition. Our immediate concern is with the nature and status of mankind as our first parents came from the hands of their Creator, what it was that constituted their fall from their initial state, and what implications that fall has had for the race of which Adam was appointed the federal head. Adam was a public person, in whose action the destiny of the race that came from him was vitally involved.

To speak of the creation is, of course, to stand counter to contemporary belief, captive as that is to the thought forms of evolutionary anthropology. The story of man as it is seen from that perspective is one of a long ascent, a saga of progress to perfectibility as social and scientific horizons broadened. The nineteenth-century concept of the perfectibility of man and the optimistic humanism of the early twentieth century, until it was shattered by war and depression as the century progressed, aided and abetted the evolutionary conceptions. But the real story of man is one of a beginning in a condition of unimaginable bliss, followed by a catastrophic fall. It is the story of a descent towards the retribution for dereliction from the demands of the covenant of creation that God had established. It is true that God has intervened, first at the very beginning in establishing a covenant of grace by which man would be rescued from the entailment of his sin; and second, by the administration of his common grace. God's immanent intervention by his common grace has been responsible for the restraint that has inhibited the fuller development of the depravity of human sin, as it is responsible also for the positive development of scientific progress and human culture.

But within the explanatory orbit of the grace of God we discover the state to which all of Adam's posterity were reduced by his fall. Why was the poet so properly exercised with "man's first disobedience, and the fruit / Of that forbidden tree whose mortal taste / Brought death into the world, and all our woe / With loss of Eden, till one greater Man / restore us, and regain the blissful seat"?[1] Or why is it said that "death reigned from Adam to Moses" (Rom 5:14), or that "in Adam all die" (1 Cor 15:22)? What is the bearing on the human condition of the apostle's summary that "by one man sin entered into the world, and death by sin," and the corollary, "all have sinned" (Rom 5:12)? The questions multiply. But man began his journey as, and notwithstanding his sin he remains, the image of God.

MAN THE IMAGE OF GOD

The trinitarian act of creation is announced in the words, "In the beginning God created" (Gen 1:1) and, of particular relevance to our present discussion, in the declarative statement, "Let us make man in our image" (Gen 1:26). The address in that text is not to be taken as directed to the angelic host, but to the Persons of the Godhead who, as we saw in the preceding chapter, were jointly engaged in the creative act. As to the creation of the angels, we do not possess correspondingly detailed advice. But there is reason to conclude that they were created at some point between the first and the sixth day of creation. Their creation occurred at some point after the "In the beginning" of Genesis 1:1. And after the creation of man on the sixth day God, it is said, reflected on all that he had made "and behold, it was very good" (Gen 1:31). Moreover, that last statement suggests that the fall of Satan, the prince of the angelic host, occurred at the end of the creation process. But then the fatal disruption that caused Satan to be cast from heaven enabled him in due course to deceive our first parents. "Ye are of your father the devil," Christ had occasion to say to the Jews, "When he speaketh a lie, he speaketh of his own: for he is a liar, and the father of it" (John 8:44).

The immediacy of the creative actions of God does not call for particular clarification. For in those actions God spoke into existence out

---

1. John Milton, *Paradise Lost,* lines 1–5.

of nothing or, we may say, *into* nothing, all of reality that came to existence external to the Godhead. No mediacy or mediating cause existed and came into play. It was not the case that "in the beginning," or at or before the beginning, there existed any material mass that provided the source from which the subsequently established universe resulted. Rather, the beginning, the point at which God created time and spoke his word into it, was the beginning. Before that there was nothing. It is true that at the beginning "the earth was without form, and void" (Gen 1:2). But that condition is not to be understood as one of complete and inexplicable chaos, without meaning or possibility of meaning. Edward J. Young, in his valuable *Studies in Genesis One*, observes that when the earth is described as initially a desolation and a waste, "This does not affirm that it was a confused mass, in the sense of being disordered and jumbled, but simply that it was not habitable, not ready for man. . . . There is no reason why God might not have pronounced the condition set forth by the first circumstantial clause of verse two as 'good.'"[2] Rather, what existed as a result of the initial creative word was precisely what God intended to exist, such that it was usable by him in the creative processes that followed. What is recorded as the creative events of the successive days of Genesis describes the divine ordering, in readiness for man's habitation, of what was at first brought into existence in the manner stated.

At the very beginning God created "the heaven and the earth." But the Scriptural record from that point on is given substantially to the affairs and issues related to the earth and to man whom God had established in it. The Scriptural concern is with the earth, and little is said of heaven. That is true apart from what in due course emerged as the promise of the coming of a redeemer who would rescue us from the entailment of sin, and the earliest consciousness in man that the promise God gave was that of eternal life. We shall return to the form and the fulfillment of that promise, but the terms of it are clear on two accounts. First, in the book of Job, probably the earliest recorded of the Old Testament Scriptures, we have the confident expectation: "I know that my redeemer liveth, and that he shall stand at the latter day upon the earth: And though after my skin worms destroy this body, yet in my flesh I shall see God" (Job 19:25–26). Second, that eschatological expectation is implicit in God's mandate to Adam that constituted the probation under which he was initially placed.

---

2. Young, *Studies in Genesis One*, 13.

It was no doubt handed down by oral transmission through patriarchal history.

The first man, Adam, was established as the vicegerent of God and as the crown of creation. He was created as the image of God. It is not sufficient to say that as he was created he *bore* the image of God. It is not simply that he is God's *image-bearer*. Rather, in his creaturehood man *is* the image of God. By reason of the image in which he is constituted, we may speak of man's *derivative personhood*. Absolute personhood exists in God, and it is because of that absolute personhood that we say that derivative personhood has been bestowed on man. That is correlative to the statement we made in the preceding chapter that because absolute knowledge and absolute meaning exist in God, the creature enjoys the possibility of derivative and analogical, but true, knowledge of the structure, purpose, and prospects of the reality-environment in which he came to self-consciousness.

What we have just referred to as man's derivative personhood implies that man himself is revelatory of God. God has revealed himself in the very constitution of man in various ways. First, by reason of man's constitutive personhood there exists a real and significant *point of contact* between man and the revelation that God has made available to him. That point of contact establishes the significance and receptivity of God's revelation, and man is accordingly without excuse for his denial of God and his obligations to him. Second, that point of contact between man and the word that God speaks rests in the correlative fact that man's derivative personhood and the image of God that it connotes carries with it a *sensus deitatis*, an ineradicable sense of God. Third, Adam's derivative personhood reveals that God is a personal God. In that, Adam's conscious possession of the faculties of thought, emotion, and will reveals that those capacities derive analogically from a *thinking, feeling, loving, purposeful, and gracious God*. Fourth, the fact that Adam immediately knew and lived in communion with God and received instructions from him is revelatory of the fact that God is a *covenant-making* God. Fifth, Adam's capacity of thought and his consciousness of truth reflected the reality that *God is himself truth*, that he speaks only and always truth, and that there is not and cannot be any contradiction in what he says and does. Sixth, the fact that God communicated to Adam all necessary criteria of action and the conditions of his probation, and the fact that the result of his dereliction was what it was, reveal that God is a *God of inviolable justice*. Finally, man's consciousness of the moral dimension of his existence reveals to him that *God is a moral agent*, of whose moral rectitude man's own morality is the replica or analogue.

In short, man is the image of God in every way in which it is possible for a finite personal creature to be like the infinite God. We offer a definition of the image of God in the following terms:

> Man, created soul and body, male and female, is the *image of God* in that he is *an immortal, rational, spiritual, moral,* and *speaking* person, capable of *reflective self-awareness* and *purposive action*, characterized in his created condition by *knowledge* and by *constitutive holiness and righteousness*, and endowed with the capacity for the reception of divine revelation, social relations and communication, and communion with God his Creator.[3]

We have spoken of the image of God in what might be said to be a broader sense. Theologians have referred to the image of God in a narrower sense, meaning by that, as our definition implies and as is stated in the Scriptures, that man is created in knowledge, righteousness, and holiness. The initial state of the image of God is there projected back from what is stated regarding the "new man" that comes to being as a result of God's grace of regeneration: "[T]he new man, which after God is created in *righteousness* and true *holiness*" (Eph 4:24), and "[T]he new man, which is renewed in *knowledge* after the image of him that created him" (Col 3:10). But the meaning of the image of God as we have stated it enables it to be seen, as will follow in a moment, that after the fall into sin, and after the effects of the fall on the faculties of the soul have been taken into account, man remains the image of God and sustains accountability to him. For man's derivative personhood has not been destroyed. He remains an immortal, spiritual, rational, moral, and speaking person.

Consider the faculties of the soul, the mind or the intellectual faculty, the affective faculty, and the will or the volitional faculty. In his pristine state Adam knew God, he freely willed to do the will of God, and he reached out to God with affection consistent with his created state of analogical being. He naturally knew, loved, and obeyed God. That follows from the fact that Adam was, as has been stated, created in a state of holiness. When that is said, it is meant that our first parent was not created in a state of moral neutrality, or in some kind of neutral tension such that

---

3. See Vickers, *Christian Confession*, 38–63.

tendencies to both good and evil were inherent in him. He was, to the contrary, constitutionally holy. He was not first created and then made the recipient of the gift of holiness, a *donum superadditum* (a gift-added-on), as certain theologies have claimed.[4] Such an erroneous doctrine has implications for the doctrine of Adam's fall that will engage us below. For it implies that when man fell, all that happened was that he lost the gift of holiness that had previously been given to him.[5] He was thereby reduced again to the state in which he existed before he had received the gift of holiness in the first place. That means that man as he exists in the state of sin after the fall possesses not only the faculties of soul, but also the capacities and abilities of those faculties that he had as he was originally created. But as will be seen, the Scriptures require us to hold a much more radical and far reaching explanation of sin. Sin affected the faculties of the soul in a more radical way than such an erroneous doctrine of man's creation contemplates.

Adam was, as created, in possession of all necessary ability to continue in the condition of holiness and righteousness with which, as the image of God, he had been endowed. But while he was constitutively holy, he was mutable, defectible, and capable of falling into sin by repudiating the covenantal obligations that his creation imposed upon him. As is only too well known, "Our first parents, being left to the freedom of their own will, fell from the estate wherein they were created, by sinning against God."[6]

We have said that man as created is *rational*. That is to say, as the image of God he thinks because God thinks, just as it follows that he speaks because God speaks. He is endowed with the faculty of speech in order that, in the first place, he can understand and respond to the speech of God to him; and secondly, in order that he can have social communication and thereby contribute to the investigation, understanding, and development of reality that the creation mandate from God entrusted to him. For Adam in his initial state, the mind was the prince of the faculties of the soul. Because it is as the image of God that he thinks, in his original and prelapsarian state he was able to think truly. That is, he was capable

---

4. See, for example, the theology of Roman Catholicism. See Berkhof, *Systematic Theology*, 208.

5. Referring to Aquinas' doctrine Van Til observes that its essence implies that at the fall man "lost the *donum superadditum*," *Reformed Pastor*, 103.

6. Westminster Shorter Catechism, Question 13.

of thought in a manner that reflected the laws of thinking that God impressed on the human soul.

When we say that man in his initial state was able to reason correctly, consistently with the laws of thought (for he was in that state sinless, meaning that he had not yet transgressed the laws of God, including the laws of thought), we nevertheless agree with John Frame's observation that "[E]ven a perfect creaturely knowledge ... would be a limited knowledge."[7] In that, we have an instance of the need not to confuse finitude and sin. But Frame, in a section headed "Limitations on Our Knowledge of God," argues that "an honest mistake is not sinful in itself" and concludes that "Unfallen Adam ... might have made ... mistakes, even about theological formulations."[8] If, as we have argued, Adam was established as the image of God, with all that implies regarding his initially endowed knowledge, holiness, and righteousness, his theological perceptions and understandings, though they were not at first tarnished by sin, would necessarily be incomplete by reason of his finitude. But as to his knowledge of God, they were nevertheless true. In his primeval state Adam knew correctly and truly (though not comprehensively), and that true knowledge was, in the nature of his position and status, open to progressive development.

We have said also that as he was created Adam was a *moral agent*. In his very constitution man is innately aware, as was Adam, that he sustains covenantal obligations to God. In Adam's case, that covenantal obligation carried with it the dual prospects of blessing or curse as they depend on either obedience or disobedience respectively. Because one *knows* the truth, he is thereby under obligation to *obey* the truth, or to conform his actions and behavior to the implications of the truth. In his prelapsarian state Adam did precisely that. He knew that the God from whose hands he came was his lawgiver.

But the principal consideration now at issue is that Adam did not sustain the estate in which he had been created. As we consider our first parents' probation and their sin, it will be seen that an *immediate* act of God imputed the guilt of that sin to the entire human race that followed. Our argument is that a substitution of *mediacy* for that divine act of im-

---

7. Frame, *Doctrine of the Knowledge of God*, 21.

8. Ibid., 20–21. See the review of Frame's *Doctrine of the Knowledge of God* by Mark Karlberg, "On the Theological Correlation of Divine and Human Language," 99–105. See also Frame's rejoinder in his *Doctrine of God*, 751.

mediate imputation amounts to a misdirection of the church's theology at a critically important point.

THE ADAMIC PROBATION

God's speech to Adam in his created state, as explicitly stated in the Genesis record, was threefold. It included a mandate regarding Adam's work obligation and the development of human culture, a provision for his on-going support, and a prohibition regarding certain actions and the institution of a probation that was associated with it. Our principal concern is with the third such word from God.

As to what has been referred to as the creation mandate, God commissioned our first parents in the following terms: "Be fruitful, and multiply, and replenish the earth, and subdue it: and have dominion over the fish of the sea, and over the fowl of the air, and over every living thing that moveth upon the earth" (Gen 1:28). Adam was established as God's vicegerent, and in that capacity delegated responsibilities as prophet, priest, and king were entrusted to him. He was to discharge the office of prophet in that he was to investigate, discover, and explain the meaning of the reality-environment in which he had been placed. As priest he was to dedicate back to God the meaning and explanatory significance of all he discovered and in terms of which he then conducted his life. And as king he was to rule over all of reality to the glory of his Maker. He had begun to discharge those offices in his prelapsarian state, at the same time as he was the beneficiary of further revelation and instructions from God as he walked with him "in the garden in the cool of the day" (Gen 3:8). When, for example, God brought all the creatures to him, "whatsoever Adam called every living creature, that was the name thereof" (Gen 2:19). But it was in due course a significant part of the meaning of Adam's fall that he thereby surrendered the capacity to discharge the offices of prophet, priest, and king.

Second, it was a part of God's administration of his common grace that he gave to Adam, as he did to the lesser creatures, their necessary food provision. It is true that what Adam was told he was to eat (Gen 1:29–30) would become available as a result of the work he was to do in cultivating the earth. The mandate of work did not wait until after his fall. It was part of the creatively structured scheme of things. But it is true that as a result of the fall the relation between man and the earth was dramatically changed. The earth would henceforth give its produce grudgingly. Adam was told that "cursed is the ground for thy sake; in sorrow shalt thou eat of it all the days of thy life ... In the sweat of thy face shalt thou eat bread" (Gen 3:17–19). But work as such, and therefore the nobility and privilege of work, is to be carefully guarded as a creation mandate.

Third, in the luxuriance of the Garden of Eden two trees were specifically designated as having particular significance, the tree of life and the tree of the knowledge of good and evil (Gen 2:9). Our first parents were permitted to eat of every tree in the garden except that of the knowledge of good and evil. It is of particular significance, therefore, that Adam was permitted to eat of the tree of life. That was because that tree was accorded a unique sacramental significance. Eating of it was a sacrament that served to Adam as a confirmation of the promise of eternal life that God had made to him. The terms of that promise will be referred to more expansively in a moment.

But it has been argued by some theologians that Adam did not partake of the tree of life prior to his fall, such a claim being based on the fact that following the fall Cherubims were placed at the garden to prevent Adam's access to it. The reason for forbidding access, as the record states, was that Adam should thereby be prevented from eating of the tree of life in the mistaken belief that by doing so he could attain eternal life (Gen 3:22). A brief comment on such claims is in order.

Our first parents had made the mistake of imagining that by eating of the forbidden tree of the knowledge of good and evil they could thereby acquire a status superior to what, as they were misled to believe, God had initially accorded them. The tempter had told them that if they ate of the tree their eyes would be opened and they would be as gods (Gen 3:5). They ate, and they became like God, but in only one respect, namely that they were thereby confirmed in moral character. But the subtlety in the result and the damning nature of the outcome was that the moral character in which they were confirmed was evil. Now, following the fall, in a statement of divine irony God said that they might conceivably make a similar mistake of proceeding on false expectations if, in their fallen state, they again ate of the tree of life. God therefore took steps to prevent such an error. Our first parents' exclusion from the sacrament of the tree of life following their sin is reflected in the present day administration of the church where similar exclusion from the sacrament of the Lord's

Supper may follow in the course of discipline where that must necessarily be administered by the church.

Leaving aside a quite extensive argument on the point in the theological literature, the conclusion of Francis Turretin, a seventeenth-century successor to Calvin in Geneva, is relevant. "It [the tree of life] was a sacrament and symbol of the immortality which would have been bestowed upon Adam if he had persevered in his first state. Augustine says, 'He had nourishment in other trees; in this, however, a sacrament.' . . . As often as he tasted its fruit, he was bound to recollect that he had life not from himself, but from God. With respect to future life, it was a declarative and sealing sign of the happy life to be passed in paradise and to be changed afterwards into a heavenly life, if he had continued upright."[9]

God's statement to Adam regarding the tree of the knowledge of good and evil constituted the probation under which Adam was placed. "But of the tree of the knowledge of good and evil, thou shalt not eat of it: for in the day that thou eatest thereof thou shalt surely die" (Gen 2:17). It was not the case that Adam was to be denied any knowledge of evil for ever. For evil had already invaded the universe in Satan's fall. The angels, who had also been created as the image of God as immortal, spiritual, rational, and moral beings, were conceivably aware of the fact of the existence of evil, though the "elect angels" (1 Tim 5:21) had not themselves sinned. And Adam was given the conditional promise of eternal heavenly life in which he would be present with the angelic host at the throne of God. What was at issue, rather, was that God imposed on Adam a test of morality, a test that implied that the way to knowledge that would be fully open to him was a matter of God's design, not a matter of the access that the tree of knowledge might have been thought to provide.

The statement that God's prohibition of Adam's access to the tree of the knowledge of good and evil constituted in itself a statement of probation implies that if Adam had not eaten of the tree he would have been confirmed in eternal life. That is the other side, not explicitly stated in the record, of the divine statement. Eating of the tree, and, notably, thereby acting in precise disobedience of God's command, would mean death. Refraining from eating, to the contrary, would mean life. In the terms thus established we say more broadly that there came into existence thereby what has been referred to as a covenant of works. That covenant stated,

---

9. Turretin, *Institutes*, vol. 1, 581.

in other words, that in the event of Adam's obedience to the obligations implicit in the covenant, namely obedience to the promulgated law of God, he would be rewarded with eternal life. In the event of disobedience, he would be exposed to eternal perdition and separation from God.[10] Those relations are inherent in the nature of all of God's covenantal dealings with man. Obedience carries with it the prospect of life and reward. Disobedience carries with it the prospect of death and perdition. The very nature of covenantal relations is such that they contain the conditional promise of blessing and benediction in response to obedience, and that of curse and malediction in response to disobedience. It is beyond our present objectives to trace out the manner in which that twofold conditional promise, of benediction or malediction, is inherent in all of God's covenants with man.

The statement that the prohibition that God gave to Adam regarding the tree of the knowledge of good and evil involved also a conditional promise of life does not depend only on the parity of reasoning that we have noted. For as will be seen more expansively in the following chapter, the meaning of God's redemptive covenant is that in view of the entailment of sin under which all people lie as a result of Adam's fall, those whom God chose to redeem are rescued from that entailment by the substitutionary work of Christ. It is clearly stated in the Scriptures that in response to his obedience and the faithful discharge of his messianic-redemptive assignment, Christ merited the reward in terms of which, in his human nature as in his divine nature, he was elevated to the right hand of the Father. Given, then, that Christ in his human nature merited the reward on the grounds of obedience, so the reward of eternal life would have accrued to Adam on the grounds of *his* obedience. For the first Adam was a type of the second. In that connection, Charles Hodge observed that "Had [Adam] retained his integrity he would have merited the promised blessing."[11]

The doctrine of the covenant of works in terms of which Adam's probation was constituted has been the subject of an extensive literature. Suffice it to observe for our present purposes that Hodge, in the statement we have just noted, follows a long line of Reformed theologians.

---

10. The biblical doctrine of the covenant of works has been widely discussed in the literature of the church and in recent times it has come under attack. A review of recent controversies and a defense of the doctrine is contained in Vickers, *Divine Redemption*, chapters 2 and 3.

11. Hodge, *Systematic Theology*, vol. 2, 364.

Hodge has written approvingly of Herman Witsius who, writing in the seventeenth century in what has become a classic treatment of the subject, concludes with reference to God's conditional promise to Adam that "God has, by his promises, made himself a debtor to man. Or, to speak in a manner more becoming God, he was pleased to make his performing his promises, a debt to himself, to his goodness, justice, and veracity."[12] Archibald Alexander Hodge, who succeeded his father, Charles, at Princeton Theological Seminary, stated that "Under the covenant of works, God graciously promised to reward the obedience of Adam with eternal life."[13]

THE NATURE AND EFFECTS OF ADAM'S SIN

Our first parents ate the forbidden fruit. That sin of disobedience dissolved their primeval relation to God and cast them down to the state of sin. We refer to the *state* of sin to which they were reduced because the effect of their act was to place them, as to their capacities of soul and their existential status, under captivity to the devil who had deceived them. Our Lord stated to the Jews on a memorable occasion that "Whosoever committeth sin is the servant [slave] of sin" (John 8:34). And the apostle similarly argued to the Romans that "to whom ye yield yourselves servants [slaves] to obey, his servants [slaves] ye are" (Rom 6:16).[14] Christ argued to the Jews that "When a strong man armed keepeth his palace, his goods are in peace" (Luke 11:21), meaning thereby that man in sin is the enslaved, comfortable, and peaceful dupe of the devil.

But Adam's sin was essentially his repudiation of his covenantal obligations. Those obligations required him to acknowledge that in his personhood he was the derivative analogue of God, that the knowledge he possessed was derivative knowledge, and that his holiness was a derivative holiness. The essence of his sin was that, contrary to the demands of those obligations, he asserted his autonomy from God. Of course, that assertion was a false assertion. The fact that it was false constitutes its sinfulness. It came to expression on three levels. It involved the assertion of metaphysical, epistemological, and ethical autonomy.

---

12. Witsius, *Covenants*, vol. 1, 48. See Hodge, op. cit., vol. 2, 359.
13. Hodge, *Outlines of Theology*, 528.
14. The Greek text at John 8:34 and Romans 6:16 is properly translated as "slaves."

On the first of those levels, Adam asserted that as to his being he was independent of God. In a profound sense, in his fall Adam denied his creaturehood. He was not prepared to acknowledge that by reason of the Creator-creature relation that existed, God rightly and justly demanded obedience from him. He knew that he had come from the hands of his Creator, but he decided that henceforth he was not dependent on any statement of God for the definition and explanation of himself. He would regard himself, in the same manner as a much later poet: "I am the master of my fate; / I am the captain of my soul."[15]

Second, the assertion of epistemological autonomy meant that Adam asserted that he was not dependent on God for what he knew and for his capacity for knowledge, or for the apprehension of the correct criteria of validity and truth. The devil told Adam that what God had said was not necessarily true. Adam then assumed he was faced with two contrasting options as to knowledge. God said one thing and the devil said another. What was Adam to believe and act upon? He decided that he would make his own decision, independently of the forces bearing on him. For he was now, he asserted, autonomous. He would not be bound by what either God or Satan said. He would decide for himself. That is the assertion of epistemological autonomy.

Third, because Adam asserted that he was independent of God on the levels of both being or creaturehood and knowledge, it followed that the position he took involved also the false assertion of ethical autonomy. By that claim, he asserted that he did not need to take his criteria of proper and morally correct behavior from God and from the law that God had set forth. He could, he asserted, find all necessary criteria of behavior within himself, or within the world around him. On that level again, Adam asserted his independence from God.

Adam's fall led to what has been properly described as a condition of total depravity. By that it is not meant that man in the state of estrangement from God that followed is as sinful as he might possibly be. It means that in the state of sin all of the faculties of the soul have been affected, disabled from their earlier functional capacities, and in that sense depraved. In Adam's pristine state the faculty of mind was the prince of the faculties of the soul. Now the mind was darkened. "[T]he god of this world hath blinded the minds of them that believe not" (2 Cor 4:4). The affective

---

15. Henley, *Invictus*, lines 15–16.

faculty is now turned inwards on man himself and man is, as the letter to the Romans declares, a "God-hater" (Rom 1:30). Now the harmony of the faculties has been shattered and the emotional capacity has displaced the hegemony of reason. Man as he now exists apart from the redeeming grace of God no longer does what he does because a mind that reflects the holy character of God instructs him. Now he does what he wants to do. The passions, the heart, the desires are in command. Reason has capitulated to passion in the human condition. Ignorance, guilt, and misery disguise their seductions and pretenses and degrade men's souls.

IMMEDIATE IMPUTATION

Two results have followed for the human condition from Adam's dereliction from his covenantal obligations and from the state of sin that resulted. First, the guilt of Adam's sin was imputed to, or placed to the account of, all those descending from him by ordinary generation. And second, as a result of the entrance of sin, all those descendents come into the world characterized by a fallen and sinful nature. Those two results and implications call for separate consideration, the imputation of sin on the one hand, and the transmission of sinful nature on the other. At this point our interest lies in the imputation of sin. The inevitability of sinful nature, while recognition of it will be necessary in what follows, will occupy us again in the following chapter when the question of man's response to the call of the gospel is addressed.

We have already seen that the divine arrangements at the creation were such that Adam was appointed as the federal head, or the representative head, of the race that was to come from him. If Adam had sustained his probation he would have been confirmed in holy state and would have been admitted to eternal life. The condition of his progeny would have followed accordingly. But because Adam fell, all those descending from him fell. That being so, the question at this point has to do with the manner in which the imputation of Adam's sin, precisely the guilt of his first sin, was effected. It is to that question that the preceding discussion has been intended to lead.

We have spoken of the *immediacy of God* in his being, in his knowledge, and in the exercise of his will. Now, as we reflect on God's action in imputing Adam's sin to all his posterity we ask again whether that action of God is *immediate* or *mediate*. We are asking, as before, whether there should be understood to exist any form of *mediacy*, any mediating or secondary cause, between God's intentions and actions on the one hand and the resulting effect in and on the human condition on the other. We are not here speaking of immediacy in a temporal sense. For whatever the results and effects of Adam's sin are to be understood to be, it is clear that those effects followed immediately (as to time) on the sin that was committed. Our question again has to do with the presence or otherwise of any mediating cause in what might be conjured as the process of imputation.

That God should have appointed Adam as the responsible head of the race is not the question before us. That appointment of Adam is simply the manner in which and the method by which God in his eternal wisdom structured the reality, including the reality of human nature, that he brought to existence. It is beyond our finite competence to raise any question as to God's eternal design and will. We have stated that nothing is more ultimate in the matter of explanation of any aspect of reality than the will of God. The question can never be *why* God appointed Adam as the head of the race. The question must be concerned, rather, with the implications of the fact that God has done so.

The Scriptural datum that is critically relevant to our question is the statement of Paul to the Romans, "Wherefore, as by one man sin entered into the world, and death by sin; and so death passed upon all men, *for that all have sinned*" (Rom 5:12). The italicized phrase is saying simply that when Adam sinned, all his posterity (by ordinary generation) sinned. There was not, that is to say, any mediating cause or act that involved us in sin at that point. The fact that Adam sinned meant and involved that we sinned. We sinned in Adam. That is the critical statement at issue.[16]

The Greek text at that point can be translated as "because all sinned," or "inasmuch as all sinned." The point can be put in another way. "[T]hrough the offense of one many died" (Rom 5:15). "[B]y one man's offence death reigned by [or through] one" (Rom 5:17). "[B]y the offense of one judgment came upon all men to condemnation" (Rom 5:18). "[B]y one man's disobedience many were made sinners" (Rom 5:19).

Now at that point mystery exists as to God's action in involving all individuals subsequent to Adam in his sinful act. Murray judiciously observes that "it is not ours to solve all mysteries and by no means ours to call in question the government of God in inflicting the whole race with the penal

---

16. The most important single examination of this critical doctrine is contained in Murray, *The Imputation of Adam's Sin*.

consequences of Adam's own sin."[17] But what is clearly stated is that because of Adam's act *all men thereby and immediately became sinners.*

When it is thus said that *all men became sinners* it is being said that by reason of Adam's sin all men were *constituted* sinners. That is, God at that point, and because of what had occurred at that point, regarded all men as sinners. That implies that when the state of all men in the world is brought under review, it cannot be said that they are sinners, or, that is, constituted to be sinners, because they come into the world with a fallen nature. The opposite is true. All men come into the world with a fallen nature because they were constituted sinners at the point of Adam's sin. That is because God imputed to them at that point the guilt of Adam's sin.

God's imputation of sin, then, was an *immediate*, and in no sense or respect a *mediate*, imputation. But, it can be asked, what are the possible grounds on which a claim of mediate imputation might conceivably be based, and on which it has in fact been based in the literature of the church? Any such grounds, it can be said, would involve a defective view of sin in and of itself, and it would evince a defective understanding of the entailment of sin. That becomes clear when we bear in mind again at this point that Adam's fall involved for all his posterity by ordinary generation both the imputation of the guilt of his sin and the transmission of a fallen nature. The meaning of both those realities must be accounted for in a full view of sin. With that understanding in mind, the question arises whether the transmission of the fallen nature can be, or should be, understood as the ground of the imputation of guilt. If that could be said, then it would be necessary to say that the imputation of sin was *mediate* rather than *immediate*, for the mediating cause would then be understood to be the fallenness of nature. But that would involve a defective view of sin in that it ignored the biblical statement that at Adam's fall his posterity "were made [or *constituted*, κατεστάθησαν, katestathesan] sinners" (Rom 5:19).

The question we are raising can be put in other terms. What, it can be asked, constitutes original sin as that characterizes the human condition? In his very valuable treatment of the subject John Murray points out that contrary to the conclusion we have reached, the doctrinal assumption of mediate imputation of sin has historically enjoyed significant support. Murray's refers to Josua Placeus, an early theologian at the Reformed school at Saumur, whose position on this question "exercised a

---

17. Murray, *Imputation*, 85.

profound influence on subsequent thought."[18] Placeus, Murray observes, "was understood to have taught that original sin consisted simply in the depravity derived from Adam and did not include the imputation of the guilt of Adam's first sin."[19] In the outcome of a synodical debate at the time, Placeus did agree that Adam's first sin was imputed to his posterity, but that it was "mediated through the inheritance from him of a corrupt nature."[20] But what, then, is to be said of original sin? Our conclusion, as our preceding argument has stated, is that original sin consists of the full effects of the attribution to Adam's posterity of the sin of which he was guilty in his public office. Original sin is connoted by, first, the immediate imputation of the guilt attached to that first sin, and second, by the consequent entailment of an inherited sinful nature. Both that imputation and that inheritance turn for their reality and significance on the will and purpose of God.

Our conclusion, therefore, is that the imputation of guilt and the inheritance of sinful nature deserve separate but, as is now seen, vitally related consideration. The inheritance is what it is because, as the text of the letter to the Romans makes clear, we were *constituted* sinners at Adam's fall. The imputation is prior, in the order of nature, to the fallen state inherited. The fallen nature, therefore, does not stand in a mediating position on which the imputation of sin turns.

John Murray properly rejects any such conclusion of mediate imputation, and in an extensive historical review of opinion he argues forcibly for immediate imputation.[21] He concludes that "when Paul says 'one sinned' and 'all sinned' he refers to the same sin viewed in its twofold aspect as the sin of Adam, the one man, and the sin of all his posterity."[22] It can be said by way of summary, as Murray has stated it, that for the following reasons the text of Romans 5:12–19 supports and requires the conclusion of immediate imputation. The text clearly sets in *immediate conjunction*, as we have seen, first, the sin of Adam and the *death* of all (verses 12, 15, 17). And further, the same paragraph sets in *immediate conjunction* the sin of Adam and the *condemnation* of all (verses 16, 18). Then

---

18. Murray, *Imputation*, 46.
19. Ibid., 42.
20. Idem. See Murray's extensive discussion in idem *passim* of the history of debate.
21. See Murray, op. cit., 64–70.
22. Ibid., 64–65.

finally, the paragraph sets in *immediate conjunction* the sin of Adam and the *sin* of all (verses 12, 19). In the text, then, the sin, the condemnation, and the death of all are set in immediate relation to the first sin of Adam. That conjures an immediate relation that stands alone in the absence of any determining mediacy, and it points unmistakably to the conclusion of immediate imputation. The conclusion of immediate imputation can be read in the light also of the statement in 1 Corinthians 15:22, "[I]n Adam all die." Again, all sinned in Adam.[23]

It should be borne in mind also that the paragraph in Romans 5:12–21 brings into clear focus the analogy between the federal headship of Adam over his posterity and the federal headship of Christ over those who make up his kingdom. The clear import of the text is that the first Adam is a type of the second. The analogy is set out, for example, in verse 15, where it is said that "If through the offence of one [Adam] many be dead, much more the grace of God . . . which is by one man, Jesus Christ, hath abounded unto many." The same juxtaposition of "one man's offence" and "the gift of righteousness by one, Jesus Christ" is stated in verse 17.

---

23. The question of the imputation of Adam's sin, particularly, as we have stated it, the imputation of the guilt of his first sin, has been the subject of extensive debate in the history of the church. See the survey by William Cunningham in his essay on "Calvin and Beza" in *The Reformers and the Theology of the Reformation*, 345–412. Cunningham concludes that "the direct and immediate imputation of Adam's first sin to his posterity, or the holding them as involved in the guilt of that offence, is regarded as prior in the order of nature and causality to the transmission and universal prevalence among men of a depraved moral nature" (374). He observes further that "Scripture sufficiently warrants this definite doctrine" (374–75). In the same essay Cunningham refers to the less than consistently clear attitude to the question in Jonathan Edwards' treatise on *Original Sin*, and comments on Edwards' apparent adoption of mediate imputation. See *The Works of Jonathan Edwards*, vol. 1, 143–233, and 220–27 on "The imputation of Adam's sin." Charles Hodge examined the question in his *Systematic Theology*, vol. 2, 192–97 and held to the doctrine of immediate imputation. In ibid. 210–14 Hodge discusses "Objections to the Doctrine of Mediate Imputation." See also Turretin in *Institutes*, vol. 1, 613–29, where he affirms that "the actual disobedience of Adam is imputed by an immediate and antecedent imputation to all his posterity springing from him by natural generation." Dabney has also provided a history of the debate on imputation and he dissents from the doctrine of immediate imputation held by Turretin and Hodge. See Dabney, *Discussions*, vol. 1, 253f. For modern treatments see Berkhof, *Systematic Theology*, 237–43, and Reymond, *New Systematic Theology*, 436–39. Reymond comments that "This [immediate imputation] view, held by Charles Hodge and John Murray, appears to be much more in accord with the Pauline analogy between Adam and Christ . . . in that it is the only view that does justice to both halves of that analogy."

Verse 18 repeats the "offence of one" and "righteousness of one," and in the nineteenth verse the resolution of the argument occurs in the summary statement that "as by one man's [Adam's] disobedience many were made sinners, so by the obedience of one [Jesus Christ] shall many be made righteous."

If, as is clear on the basis of adequate Scriptural data, the righteousness of Christ is placed by immediate imputation to the account of those who believe in Christ without any mediating worth or merit on their part, then by analogy back from the second to the first Adam, the imputation of the first Adam's sin becomes the subject of immediate imputation on *its* level, as the righteousness of Christ is the subject of immediate imputation on *its* level. The solidarity that exists between the Christian believer and Christ is foreshadowed in the solidarity between Adam and his posterity. In both cases the solidarity points to the immediacy of the relevant imputation.

We have already had occasion to observe that the regenerating grace of God conveys new life to the sinner by a sovereign, secret, and unsolicited act of the Spirit of God. That being so, it certainly follows, as is necessary by reason of what we have seen as the state in sin of those to whom the call of the gospel comes, that no intermediate causation, no element of mediacy, makes any contribution on the sinner's part to his redemption and his resulting union with Christ.

That immediate imputation of the righteousness of Christ that has provided the basis of the analogy we have just inspected will engage us at more length in the following chapter.

4

The Immediate Imputation of Righteousness

IT WAS STATED AT the conclusion of the preceding chapter that an analogy exists between the federal headship of Adam over the race that would come from him and the headship of Christ over those who have been called to make up his kingdom. For the first Adam was a type of the second. It followed that the immediate imputation of the guilt of Adam's sin to all his posterity established an analogy with the immediate imputation of Christ's righteousness to those who believe in him. In this chapter we shall bring together several threads of argument that have already been suggested with a view to examining more fully that last-mentioned imputation. The imputation of Christ's righteousness is clarified adequately only when it is seen to be a covenantal imputation.

The hermeneutical principle in terms of which the Scriptures are to be read is provided by the reality of God's covenantal relations with man whom he established in his own image. If one could speak with extreme care and with profound humility, it could be said that the problem that faced the Godhead in eternity was that of how any from among the offspring of Adam could be rescued from the state of sin to which they had fallen. The mystery of redemption is that the issue was settled in the predeterminate council of the Godhead in the formation of the covenant of redemption. In that intratrinitarian communication within the Godhead it was decreed that the three divine Persons should undertake respective redemptive offices by which, out of their joint operation, a chosen people would be redeemed and brought to share God's eternal glory with him. Those whom the Father elected to eternal life he gave to the Son: "[T]hine they were, and thou gavest them me" (John 17:6). And for them the Son of God was to come into the world, to keep the law of God on their behalf, and to pay the penalty of the guilt of sin to which they were exposed. God the Holy Spirit undertook to convey to those people the benefits of the redemption that Christ accomplished for them, to endow them with the gifts that Christ purchased for them, notably the gifts of repentance and faith, and to conduct them to glory.

That eternal redemptive decree having been settled, it was necessary that in order to accomplish its objectives a further and implementing covenant should be established. The parties to that covenant, the covenant of grace, were God on the one hand and the people that he had chosen to redemption as they were represented by Christ. "God . . . hath chosen us in [Christ] before the foundation of the world . . . Having predestinated us unto the adoption of children by Jesus Christ to himself, according to the good pleasure of his will" (Eph 1:4–5).

But in the history of doctrinal controversy, the subjects of God's redemptive decrees have not always been adequately and consistently defined. If it is asked, "For whom did Christ die?" in fulfilling the terms of the covenant of grace, the answer follows that he died for those whom God the Father gave to him to redeem. If it is asked, "To whom is the Holy Spirit committed to apply the benefits of Christ's redemption?" the answer is that they are those for whom Christ died. The subjects of the decrees to elect, to redeem, and to call and sanctify are thus a common and identically defined set of people. But that redemptive necessity has not always been clearly understood.

In the Arminian theology, for example, it is argued that the redemption that Christ accomplished was a universal redemption, or, that is to say, that in his death Christ paid the penalty for the sins of all individuals. Those who are then saved, it is said, who become in due time the beneficiaries of Christ's redemption, are those who, by reason of the exercise of their free will choice, believe in Christ for the forgiveness of sin. They are then the ones to whom the Holy Spirit ministers his grace. And they are the ones whom, on the grounds of God's foreknowledge of their decision to believe, he elects to eternal salvation. That divine-human relation was referred to in the preceding chapter in the discussion of the knowledge of God. Thus there emerges in the Arminian theological formulation a particular construction of God's purposes and decrees in salvation. In that scheme of things, however, a disparity emerges between the subjects of the work of Christ and the subjects of the work of the Holy Spirit. In the first case those subjects are said to be *all* people, and in the second case they are contemplated as *some* people. The necessity of insisting to the contrary can be seen by noting that if, in such a way, a wedge is driven between the *work* of Christ and the *work* of the Holy Spirit, a wedge is thereby driven between the *knowledge* of Christ and the *knowledge* of the Spirit. But further, if in any respect a wedge is driven between the *works* and the *knowledge* of the members of the divine Trinity, a wedge is thereby driven between the *being* of the Persons of the Trinity. And in that case the biblical doctrine of God has been completely destroyed.[1]

It is not necessary for our present purpose to explore that defective theology at length and in detail. Its main points can be summarized briefly for purposes of comparison with what lies ahead. The Arminian system of doctrine, following the teaching of Jacob Arminius (1560–1609), came to precise formulation in a document known as the Remonstrance of 1610 and called forth the response of the Canons of Dort (1618–1619). To summarize, the Remonstrance theology taught that God's election of certain individuals to salvation was based on their foreseen faith; that Christ's atonement was a universal atonement; that man as he exists after Adam's fall is only partially depraved and that his will, particularly as that is operative in the choice of salvation, is free; that the overture of God's grace to the sinner is resistible; and that it is possible for a true Christian believer to lapse from grace and to be eternally lost.[2] It is clear that under such assumptions and conclusions the sovereignty of man has effectively eclipsed and displaced the sovereignty of God in salvation. The Arminian theology is widely held and has a very vocal presence in the contemporary evangelical church. The assumption of the sovereignty of man dies hard.[3]

What purported to be a mediating theology between Arminianism and post-Reformation Calvinism was proposed in the late seventeenth century by Moise Amyraut (Amyraldus) of the French Reformed Academy at Saumur and gave rise to a body of teaching referred to as Amyraldianism. It was given a revival recently by Alan Clifford in his critical discussion

---

1. The doctrines associated with the Arminian controversy and their dependence on an earlier Pelagianism have been extensively discussed in the standard histories of Christian doctrine. See, for example, Cunningham, *Historical Theology*, vol. 2, 371–501. Owen, foremost among the English Puritan theologians in the seventeenth century, provides a classic dissection of Arminianism in his *The Death of Death in the Death of Christ*. The treatise by Edwards, *Freedom of the Will*, is a forthright rebuttal of the Arminian doctrine regarding the status and functional ability of the human will.

2. See the Canons of Dort, along with a comparison with other post-Reformation confessions, in Beeke and Ferguson, *Reformed Confessions Harmonized*.

3. Recall the discussion of related deviationist theologies such as Open Theism and its comparison with Arminianism in chapter 2.

of English theology in the seventeenth and eighteenth centuries.[4] In essence that doctrinal movement argues for a decree of God that led to the sacrifice of Christ for all people, followed by a further decree of election of those who believe. Christ died for all men, that is, but in the application of the benefits of his death he intercedes only for the elect.[5] But its main structure has not gained the approval and concurrence of the church that has maintained the classic Reformation theology.

THE ENTAILMENT OF SIN

The erroneous views of the atonement follow in the footsteps of an old but tenacious and dangerous error. It harks back to the claims of Pelagius in the fourth century who, in his dispute with Augustine, advanced certain defective theories regarding the status of the human will. The Pelagian theology has been treated at length by Turretin, who comments on the state of the faculty of the will by observing that "the question returns to this—whether unregenerate man still has such strength of free will as to be indifferent to good and evil and is able not to sin without the grace of regeneration. The adversaries affirm; we deny." Turretin continues, "Here we have as opponents the old and new Pelagians (who place the idol of free will in the citadel) and to make men free, make them sacrilegious."[6]

Adolf Harnack, commenting on "the principles of the Pelagian doctrine," has rightly observed that "it has made its appearance in a subtle form again and again."[7] Harnack notes in relation to the Pelagian scheme that it claims that "Everything that he [God] created is good, therefore also the creature, the law and free-will. . . . accordingly there can exist no *peccata naturalia* [sin as a matter of nature], only *peccata per accidens*. Human nature can be modified only incidentally. The most important

---

4. Clifford, *Atonement and Justification*. Clifford is actively engaged in the contemporary revival of Amyraldianism in England. His work is related to that of Kendall, *Calvin and English Calvinism*, which also dissents from classic post-Reformation Calvinism. Kendall's work attracted a very effective rejoinder and rebuttal in Paul Helm's *Calvin and the Calvinists*.

5. Kendall in *Calvin and English Calvinism*, 13, similarly argues against the mainstream of post-Reformation Reformed theology and concludes, quite mistakenly, that Calvin himself held a doctrine of universal atonement: "Fundamental to the doctrine of faith in John Calvin (1509–64) is his belief that Christ died indiscriminately for all men."

6. Turretin, *Institutes*, vol. 1, 669. See also Cunningham, on "The Pelagian Controversy," in *Historical Theology*, vol. 1, 321–58.

7. Harnack, *Outlines of the History of Dogma*, 368–69.

and best endowment of this nature is free-will."[8] Accordingly, Pelagianism argued, "Man is able to resist every sin, therefore he must do so . . . Sin always remains an affair of the will and each is punished only for his own sin. All men stand in the condition of Adam before his fall."[9]

It is clear that the Pelagian scheme, against which Augustine argued vehemently, completely misrepresents the biblical doctrine of the fall. For Pelagius, the will did not suffer damage at the fall, no fallen nature has been transmitted as a result of the fall, and every man is able by the exercise of his free will to do what is good as God mandates the good. The implication is that every man is able to turn to God at will and that individual salvation is therefore merely a matter of individual decision and competence. That implies that man is sovereign in his own salvation. In his larger multi-volume work on the *History of Dogma* Harnack refers to the Pelagian doctrine as stated at the Synod of Carthage in the year 418 as claiming that "man can be without sin and can keep the divine commands easily if he will."[10]

The upshot in the history of doctrine is that the initial Pelagianism gave rise to what can be referred to as a *Semi*-Pelagianism, as that characterized the teaching of the Roman Catholic Church at the time of the Reformation. If the statement of Paul to the Ephesians is held as biblical doctrine, that man as a result of the fall is "dead in trespasses and sins" (Eph 2:1), the Pelagians rejoin that far from being dead, the natural man is very much alive. If man is dead, dead, that is, as to spiritual competence, then salvation must be completely the result of the intervention of divine grace. But that was not the position held by the church at the time of the Reformation. The church in its pre-Reformation stance had assumed an intermediate position between the biblical data and thoroughgoing Pelagianism. It was *semi*-Pelagian. That is, man wasn't dead. He was only sick, perhaps very sick. So much so that he was indeed in need of divine grace to assist him to the embrace of salvation. By God's *congruent grace* as that came to him in his natural state he was assisted and enabled to turn from his sin and express faith in Christ. That *semi*-Pelagianism survived, notwithstanding the claims of Reformation doctrine to the contrary, to come to expression in Arminianism and to continue to present-day evangelicalism.

---

8. Ibid., 369.
9. Ibid., 370.
10. Adolf Harnack, *History of Dogma*, vol. 5, 175, quoted in Sproul, *Faith Alone*, 136.

If it is said that one's salvation is dependent simply on one's own sovereign power and action of choice, then salvation is an *autosoterism*. By that it is being said that man saves himself. If, as it has been alternatively said, it were maintained that man in his natural state is damaged in his faculties to the degree that he needs the assistance of divine grace, then it would be implied that salvation is a process of *synergism*. It would be a matter of synergistic cooperation between God and man. It would be claimed that God has done his part in making salvation available to all men by reason of the death of his Son, and that now it is left to man to do his part. But the biblical doctrine that came to full expression in the Reformation theology is that salvation is not, in the preceding sense, an *autosoterism*, and neither is it a divine-human *synergism*. Salvation is a *divine monergism*.

Our first parents' fall is to be understood, then, as having three effects on the human condition. First, as was discussed in the preceding chapter, the guilt of Adam's sin was placed to the account of all of his posterity (descending from him by ordinary generation) by *immediate imputation*. Second, the fall involved the *loss of original righteousness*, and for all men since it has meant the surrender of the ability to discharge the offices to which they had been commissioned under the initial covenant of works. Third, the fall involved the transmission to Adam's posterity of a fallen nature, a transmission that involved the corruption of man's whole nature, a state of *moral depravity*. It is the rejection of that moral depravity that has occasioned the deviations from biblical doctrine we have referred to.

The condition of depravity that the fall involved projected its effects to all of the faculties of the soul. Consider the faculty of mind, the intellectual faculty of the soul. We have it in the earliest Genesis record that "God saw that the wickedness of man was great in the earth, and that every imagination of the thoughts of his heart was only evil continually" (Gen 6:5). And the apostle to the Gentiles stated that "the god of this world hath blinded the minds of them which believe not" (2 Cor 4:4). The matter at issue at that point is the ability or otherwise of the natural man to see or know or understand the meaning of the things of God. The case is underlined by the apostle: "[T]he natural man receiveth not the things of the Spirit of God: for they are foolishness unto him: neither can he know them, because they are spiritually discerned" (1 Cor 2:14). As to the affective or the emotional faculty of the soul: "The heart is deceitful above all things, and desperately wicked" (Jer 17:9). The primeval love of God has been displaced not only by a love of self, but by a hatred of God: "haters of God ... Without understanding, covenantbreakers" (Rom 1:30–31). As to the will, the volitional faculty of the soul: "Ye are of your father the devil, and the lusts of your father ye will do" (John 8:44). The Scriptural data could be multiplied.

The confessional statement gets at the heart of the matter in short compass: "Man, by his fall into a state of sin, hath *wholly lost all ability of will* to any spiritual good accompanying salvation; so as a natural man, being altogether averse from that good, and dead in sin, is not able, by his own strength, to convert himself, or to prepare himself thereunto."[11]

In short, the soul, after and as a result of the fall, is altogether and implacably turned against God. We saw in an earlier chapter that every man naturally knows *that* God is, by reason of the testimony of the *sensus deitatis* inherent in the human consciousness. But now, in the darkened entailment of sin, man no longer knows *who* God is. Two things are to be said. First, as a result of the diminished human condition following the fall, the faculties of the soul are affected by the depravity we have just observed. The soul is now *deprived* of the holiness that characterized it at the creation, and it is *depraved* by reason of the disabilities now imposed on it. Second, now the harmony of the faculties has been shattered.[12] The mind, the intellectual faculty, is no longer the prince of the faculties of the soul. The soulish condition is beyond doubt a sorry one. The more is it clear that redemption must turn on the sovereign and unsolicited grace of God.

THE FREEDOM OF THE WILL

But the status and capacities of the human will call for further consideration. Two issues are relevant. First, in the light of what has been said of the disabilities of the faculties of the soul, what is to be said of the activity of the will in the individual's progress to salvation? And second, can it in any sense be said that the will is "free," or what, that is, is the relevance of the long historic debate regarding the freedom of the will? We take the last question first.

---

11. Westminster Confession of Faith, IX:3, italics added.

12. The original state of harmony among the faculties is observed by Turretin in his comment that man as created was characterized by "wisdom in the mind, holiness in the will, and rectitude and good order in the affections. It bespeaks ... a *harmony* among the faculties." Turretin, *Institutes*, vol. 1, 466, italics added.

Having regard to the faculties of the soul as they characterize human personhood, meaning by that man in general and not yet speaking exclusively of the regenerate individual, the constitution of the soul is such that the will does not and cannot perform an uninstructed act. The will acts in accordance with what is conveyed to it as instruction from the intellectual and emotional faculties. With that acknowledgment in view, Luther asks, "[W]hat can the will pursue, when reason can propose to it nothing but the darkness of its own blindness and ignorance? Where reason is in error and the will turned away, what good can man attempt to perform?"[13] Jonathan Edwards, whose eighteenth-century work, *Freedom of the Will*, marked him as arguably the foremost philosopher-theologian that America produced, makes the point in the observation that is central to that work: "[E]very act of the will is some way connected with the understanding, and is as the greatest apparent good is."[14] Edwards' work was written as a forcible rejection of "the Arminian notion of freedom, that the will influences, orders, and determines itself."[15] Recalling our earlier comments on the Arminian notion of the freedom of the will, a contemporary scholar, Conrad Cherry, comments that "the essay *Freedom of the Will* was intended to reduce the arguments of the Arminians to absurdity."[16] In that work Edwards argues that "It is . . . impossible for the will to choose contrary to its own . . . preponderating inclination."[17] There is, Edwards claims, no "freedom of will" lying in the power of the will to determine itself."[18] Looking in the manner we have seen to the fallen characteristics of the faculties of the soul, he concludes that the explanation of the action of the will as it now exists by nature lies in "a certain deformity in the nature of the dispositions and acts of the heart."[19] Light is thrown on this whole question by Edwards' statement that the explanation of man's willing action is grounded in "the total depravity and corruption of man's

---

13. Luther, *Bondage of the Will*, 281.
14. Jonathan Edwards, op. cit., Morgan, PA edition, 86.
15. Ibid., 45.
16. Cherry, *Theology of Jonathan Edwards*, 160.
17. Edwards, *Bondage*, Morgan, PA edition, 73.
18. Ibid., 329.
19. Ibid., 341.

nature, whereby his heart is wholly under the power of sin."[20] That is the source of man's "fixed bias and inclination."[21]

If, then, we hold to the proposition that the will is not free in an isolated sense to determine its own action, but that it necessarily acts in conformity with the state, decisions, and motivations of the faculties of the soul, we may reflect on the status of the will in Adam's prelapsarian state. There existed in that state an undisturbed harmony among the faculties. The soul was then characterized by free will in the fullest sense. As to man's initial condition, Turretin noted that the probationary directive that God gave to Adam, that he should not eat of the tree of the knowledge of good and evil, was itself "necessary ... to declare that man was created by him [God] with free will; for if he had been without it, he would not have imposed such a law upon him."[22] The Westminster Shorter Catechism makes the point. When our first parents were "left to the freedom of their own will" they "fell from the estate wherein they were created."[23] That initial state of free will existed because the mind, the intellectual faculty, naturally knew God and responded with clarity and uncluttered reason to the knowledge of God that was inherent in Adam's created condition. At the same time, with the affective or emotional faculty Adam naturally loved God, and that natural disposition, the *habitus* implicit in the soul, moved our first parent to love the law of God and to love the work of obedience. In harmonious concurrence, then, the will was naturally instructed to obey God. There was at that time no discordance or possibility of disruption among the faculties so long as the initial state of righteousness was preserved.[24]

A highly significant sense exists, therefore, in which it can be said that at the fall man lost his free will. Certainly we have seen that as a result of the fall he is disabled from the initial functions and prerogatives with which he was created. But as to action in general, and apart from the precise question of the knowledge of God and actions in accordance with the mandates of God, the question persists whether there exists any respect in which the will can be said to be free. Our response must be that in all respects, and by the very nature of the constitution of the soul and

20. Ibid., 325.
21. Ibid., 321.
22. Turretin, *Institutes*, vol. 1, 579–80.
23. Westminster Shorter Catechism, Question 13.
24. See the discussion in Cunningham, on "The Doctrine of the Will," in *Historical Theology*, vol. 1, 568–639.

human personhood, the will remains under the inevitable influence of the intellectual and emotional deliberations. When Edwards said that the action of the will is "as the greatest apparent good is," he was laying down a principle which, of necessity, is universally explanatory of willing action. For example, a man may well have decided at one time or another that excessive consumption of alcohol is a thing which, on the basis of his own established moral principles, he will avoid. But if, on a certain occasion, he takes alcohol to an excess and thereby defies what he had previously laid down as a moral principle, it is not to be said that he is doing so against his will. Nor can it properly be said that his will is free, in an isolated and independent sense, to take the alcohol or not take it. The situation in strict reality is that he took the alcohol because, at the point of taking it, it was apparent to him that that action was, in the situation that existed, "his greatest apparent good." His reason and his emotional preferences at that time dictated that the preponderance of good rested in the action he then took. The action of taking the alcohol was not an independent act of the will. It was an act of the whole person.

In the light of the conjunction of the faculties of the soul in the determination of action it is apposite to make a brief comment on the status of human reason. In particular, it would be a mistake to conclude from what has been said that in the fall any of the faculties have been destroyed in the sense of their being disabled from normal and general function. The faculties of reason and emotion, for example, have not been destroyed, but they have been made subject, as we have seen, to a bias that is constituted by the entailment of sin. Van Til made a significant contribution to the discussion in his statement that "Metaphysically, both parties [the believer and the non-believer] have all things in common, while epistemologically they have nothing in common."[25] Both parties exist in and share a common reality, the reality that God spoke into existence. But their ways of knowing, in the sense of the presuppositions on the ground of which they reason, the validity criteria of truth that they hold, and therefore the end result of their knowledge processes, are different. It is true that the laws of logic are the same for the believer and the unbeliever, and it is not true that the rules of the syllogism are different for the Christian and

---

25. Van Til, *Common Grace*, 5.

the non-Christian. "The unbeliever can follow the technical processes of intellectual procedure as well as, or often better than, the believer."[26]

As to the structure and procedures of unregenerate thought, of scientific thought for example, the epistemic difference can be put in Van Til's conclusion: "It is either the would-be autonomous man, who weighs and measures what he thinks of as brute or bare facts by the help of what he thinks of as abstract impersonal principles, or it is the believer, knowing himself to be a creature of God, who weighs and measures what he thinks of as God-created facts by what he thinks of as God-created laws."[27] Abraham Kuyper has similarly spoken of "The Twofold Development of Science," in the course of which he refers to "two kinds of people" and "two kinds of science." By that he distinguishes the scientific work of those who are, by the grace of God, regenerate believers and those who remain unregenerate. Kuyper adduces as a distinguishing benchmark that differentiates the respective epistemic processes what he refers to as *palingenesis*, or the grace of regeneration.[28]

THE REGENERATE WILL

On a memorable occasion that is reported in each of the synoptic gospels (Matt 19:16–26; Mark 10:17–27; Luke 18:18–27) a certain young man enquired earnestly of Jesus as to what he should do in order to inherit eternal life. We are arrested by our Lord's exchange with his disciples following the young man's rejection of the response he had received. With a certain confusion and amazement the disciples asked, "Who then can be saved?" The reply Christ gave strikes to the heart of the meaning of salvation. "With men this is impossible; but with God all things are possible." If any are saved it is the result, not of any exercise of inherent human capacities, but of the sovereign action of God and his conveyance to the soul of the benefits of the redemption that Christ accomplished. That divinely ordered process now engages us.

The covenant of grace, the accomplishment of whose objectives was necessary to the realization of the divine purpose of redemption, was announced to our first parents following their fall into sin. The announcement, at the same time as it declared the wrath of God against Satan and

---

26. Ibid., 27.
27. Ibid., 44.
28. Kuyper, *Principles of Sacred Theology*, 150ff.

sin, projected God's purpose to the coming of Christ as the redeemer. "I will put enmity between thee and the woman," God said to Satan, "and between thy seed and her seed; it shall bruise thy head, and thou shalt bruise his heel" (Gen 3:15). There we have the *protoevangelium*, the first statement of the gospel, the promise that Christ the redeemer would come.

That initial statement of the promise of redemption was expanded in due course as successive forms of administration of the covenant of grace followed. After the patriarchal period of history, when the substance of the promise was kept alive by oral transmission, God called Abraham and renewed the promise to him. The Mosaic and Davidic histories followed to the same effect. Paul takes up the history and sharpens the focus uniquely on Christ in his explanatory statement to the Galatian church. "[T]o Abraham and his seed were the promises made. He saith not, And to seeds, as of many; but as of one, And to thy seed, which is Christ" (Gal 3:16).

But what is to be said, then, of the work that Christ did in fact accomplish, and why could it be said that it pointed to the redemption of those whom God had covenantally given to him to redeem? To consider the answer in what is no doubt an inadequately condensed form we reflect again on the meaning of our first parents' fall. Two aspects of that are immediately relevant. First, in his fatal assertion of autonomy Adam had repudiated the covenantal obligations to which he was committed under the covenant of works. Those obligations required that he should obey the probationary mandate that God had given him and that, continuing in a state of holiness, he should discharge the offices of prophet, priest, and king. Adam's fall shattered the pristine divine-human relation and the obligations of the covenant of works remained unfulfilled. Second, as a result of Adam's dereliction from his covenantal status he was not only disabled in all the faculties of soul, but he stood under the wrath of God against sin and under the consequent prospect of the penalty of eternal perdition.

As we contemplate the work of Christ we observe a crucial relation to those two aspects of the fall. In the first place, it is not correct to assume that "Man's sin destroyed the creation covenant,"[29] or that "Adam's disobedience . . . ended the covenant of creation."[30] For following the fall, the obligations of that covenant continued, and all persons everywhere

29. Vande Kapelle and Currid, "The Old Testament: The Covenant Between God and Man" in Hoffecker, ed., *Building a Christian World View*, 25.

30. Beale and Bibza, "The New Testament: The Covenant of Redemption in Jesus Christ," in ibid., 49.

remain under responsibility to its terms. It is to be said of the work of Christ that on that first level he came to do for us what we were obligated to do under the covenant of works but what, by reason of our involvement in sin, we were unable to do for ourselves. Christ fulfilled for us our unfulfilled obligations under the covenant of works. As to the relations involved, A. A. Hodge has commented that "This Covenant having been broken by Adam, not one of his natural descendants is ever able to fulfill its conditions, and Christ having fulfilled all of its conditions in behalf of all his own people . . . the Covenant of Works having been fulfilled by the second Adam is henceforth abrogated under the gospel. Nevertheless, since it is founded upon the principles of immutable justice, *it still binds all men* who have not fled to the refuge offered in the righteousness of Christ."[31] Reymond has observed that all people "are still culpable before God and subject to death on the basis of the original covenant of works."[32] It is not being said that the covenant of works remains as a way of eternal life as was the case in Adam's initial state. It is that the sinner in his natural state remains exposed to the curse that dereliction from the covenant contemplated. But in his coming, Christ kept the law of God perfectly on our behalf and he came as the perfect prophet, priest, and king to whom all of history had pointed. He was our substitute in those vital and necessary respects.

All that Christ did in fulfilling the demands of the law is frequently referred to as his active obedience. It is to be realized, however, that there was decidedly what may be called a passive aspect of his active obedience, in that he voluntarily submitted himself to obedience to the Father. For he came, he said, "not to do mine own will, but the will of him that sent me" (John 6:38). Again, his work in dying on the cross as the substitute for sinners is referred to as his passive obedience. But there was a decidedly active aspect to his passive obedience. For he made it clear that "I lay down my life, that I might take it again. No man taketh it from me, but I lay it down of myself. I have power to lay it down, and I have power to take it again" (John 10:17–18).

As to the second of the implications of Adam's fall, his liability to punishment for sin, Christ came to be our substitute in paying in his death the penalty that was due to us. In his life in this world Christ dis-

---

31. Hodge, *Outlines of Theology*, 314, italics added.
32. Reymond, *New Systematic Theology*, 439.

charged the offices of the final and perfect prophet, priest, and king, the antitype of all the Old Testament types that had anticipated and pointed to him in those capacities. As prophet he made God the Father known to us, he "declared" God to us (John 1:18), and he revealed to us the will of God for our salvation. Moreover, he reversed the loss of the principles of interpretation that Adam suffered in the fall, and he gave to us a new understanding of the true criteria of knowledge, wisdom, and truth on all levels of intellection. "[W]here shall wisdom be found?" Job had asked, or "Whence then cometh wisdom? and where is the place of understanding?" (Job 28:12, 20). But in Christ "are hid all the treasures of wisdom and knowledge" (Col 2:3). Christ, in his coming and in the revelation he gave, made possible not only the moral renewal of those he came to save, but also, significantly, their epistemic renewal. As king he came to establish a rule over his people, the church over which he is the Head, a messianic kingdom that he will at the last time give back to the Father (1 Cor 15:24). When the Jews on one occasion complained against him that he was casting out devils by the power of Beelzebub, the chief of the devils, he rejoined against that blasphemy by saying that "if I with the finger of God cast out devils, no doubt the kingdom of God is come upon you" (Luke 11:20).

As the great high priest Christ came as the antitype of the Levitical priesthood in that he made the one final and complete offering for sin. It was necessary, as the letter to the Hebrews is eloquent in declaring, that those older sacrifices should be offered regularly, including that on the annual Day of Atonement (Leviticus 16). But while, with all those sacrifices, "it is not possible that the blood of bulls and of goats should take away sins" (Heb 10:4), and the Levitical priests were "offering oftentimes the same sacrifices, which can never take away sins" (Heb 10:11), "this man [Christ] ... offered one sacrifice for sins for ever ... by one offering he hath perfected for ever them that are sanctified" (Heb 10:12, 14). The older sacrifices, to the extent that they were offered by those who came to the altar in true faith, effected a ceremonial cleansing. They were efficacious in according pleasure to God, and the offering accrued to the spiritual benefit of the one who brought it, when it was brought in faith in the veracity of God in his promise that a Savior would come to provide the true and final atonement for sin. But then in due time, in the sacrifice of Christ he was both the offering and the priest who gave the offering.

For in the satisfaction for sin that he provided he gave himself. Not any longer "the blood of bulls and of goats . . . Christ offered himself without spot to God" (Heb 9:13–14).

The question now arises as to how one is "made partaker of the redemption purchased by Christ."[33] The answer follows that the Spirit of God applies that redemption and thereby conveys to the believer the benefits of it, "by working faith in us, and thereby uniting us to Christ in our effectual calling."[34] The biblical doctrine of effectual calling provides us with an entry to the answer of the question before us regarding the status of the will in the regenerate individual. "Effectual calling is the work of God's Spirit, whereby, convincing us of our sin and misery, enlightening our minds in the knowledge of Christ, and *renewing our wills*, he doth persuade and enable us to embrace Jesus Christ freely offered to us in the gospel."[35] When we considered earlier the fact that in the fall all of the faculties of the soul were depraved, it was stated that there could be no reconciliation between God and the sinner because the latter was alienated from God in a blindness of mind, a perversity and hatred of heart, and a deadened will so far as the things of God were concerned. What we now have in view as the Spirit of God's effectual calling demonstrates and effects a reversal of precisely those disabilities.

That is so in the sense that the calling "enlightens the mind," thereby reversing the blindness in which the god of this world (2 Cor 4:4) has bound the sinner. It "convinces of sin and misery," so that with a renewal of the affective and emotional faculties one is now able to agree with God's statement of his true condition in sin, and it "renews our wills" to the effect that one is now able to "embrace Jesus Christ." Here, in the grace of effectual calling conveyed to the sinner in accordance with God's purpose of election, we see the complete reversal of the state to which all people had fallen by reason of Adam's sin.

The seventeenth-century terminology (in what we have just cited from the Westminster Shorter Catechism) has given place in theological vocabulary to the doctrine of regeneration. Or it can be said that what is referred to as regeneration is properly understandable as an aspect of the more comprehensive rubric of effectual calling as the Catechism has

---

33. Westminster Shorter Catechism, Question 29.
34. Ibid., Question 30.
35. Ibid., Question 31, italics added.

stated it. For the doctrine of regeneration as such focuses particularly on the effects on the soul of the renewing work of the Holy Spirit and leaves the expression of saving faith to a subsequent doctrinal formulation. But what, then, is to be understood as regeneration, and in what respect does that answer our question regarding the status of the regenerate will?

We may respond by saying that regeneration is that sovereign, secret, and unsolicited work of the Holy Spirit within the soul whereby the faculties of the soul are endowed with capacities and abilities they did not previously possess, and by which a new disposition or principle of action is embedded in the soul. We say that the Spirit's act of regeneration is sovereign. That is necessarily the case because the individual to whom the Spirit comes is, before and at the time of his coming, dead in sin. That is clear from previous consideration of the natural state of the soul. If regeneration were not a sovereign awakening, the soul would remain in its slumbering captivity to sin. The Spirit's act of regeneration, it has been said further, is unsolicited. That is again necessarily true because when the individual is dead in sin he cannot in any sense request, by the exercise of his own will, the presence of the Spirit of God. But what is to be said of the resulting effects on the faculties of the newly regenerate soul?

It is of principal interest to our present question that a new endowment has been conveyed to the will that was previously directed implacably against God. The will, in short, to repeat the catechism, is "renewed." We recall previous discussion under the heading of what is to be said of the freedom or otherwise of the will. It would at this point be a mistake of the highest order to suggest that the work of the Holy Spirit is in any sense a violation of individual freedom of will. For we have seen that the will, in its action, is subject to, and is under the collective guidance of, the faculties of the soul. That remains the case. But now those faculties have been the subject of new endowments. Now the natural darkness of the mind has been abolished and the individual is able to see and understand what was always there to be seen but was hidden from him. Now, in the light of that new endowment, he is able to consent to what God has said is the truth regarding his status and position. It is thus an essential aspect of the saving faith with which he has been newly endowed ("by grace are ye saved through faith; and that not of yourselves: it is the gift of God" [Eph 2:8]) that he assents to God's declaration of his case. And now the affective and emotional faculty that previously labeled the sinner as a "hater of God" (Rom 1:30) naturally seeks after God in a longing to know him.

Because it is now the renewed faculties that are guiding and instructing the will, the will is in no sense violated. Rather, the will is made willing in a new sense, consistent with a new soulish disposition, to seek after and obey God. The Psalmist has stated that "Thy people shall be willing in the day of thy power" (Ps 110:3).

The contrasting cases can be put as follows: "Man, by his fall into a state of sin, hath *wholly lost all ability of will*, to any spiritual good accompanying salvation."[36] "Hence the necessity," as Cunningham has stated, "not only of the conviction of sin and the illumination of the understanding, *but also of the renovation of the will*, in order to men's embracing Christ."[37] It remains only to be said that in the work of the Holy Spirit in the soul there is, in addition to the renewing of the mind and the affections, a positive strengthening also of the will. Thus, because all of the faculties are benefited by the Spirit's work and intervention, the individual who is now a new person in Christ is able to, and he or she does, commit to Christ in a whole-souled belief and trust.

IMMEDIATE IMPUTATION

In the Holy Spirit's conveyance to the individual of the grace of regeneration certain spiritual effects are thereby produced. First, the gifts of repentance and saving faith are imparted, and associated with the assent by the renewed soul to the truth of what God has declared, a whole-souled commitment in trust to Christ as Savior follows. Second, as the apostle explained to the Corinthians, there occurs at that time a baptism by the Spirit into the body of the church, confirming the individual's membership of the church in its invisible aspect which Christ set out to redeem (1 Cor 12:13). Third, what the apostle referred to in his Ephesian letter as the sealing of the Spirit occurs (Eph 1:13), and the new-born person is marked as a child of God. And fourth, at the point of regeneration the individual who is the beneficiary of that grace is joined to Christ in a vital and indissoluble union. Our interest in this final section, leaving aside discussion of many aspects of what has just been said, centers on the grounds on which, in response to the individual's exercise of the saving faith that the Spirit has conveyed to him, God declares the sinner forgiven of sin and established in a state of reconciliation with him. At that point the individual

---

36. Westminster Confession of Faith, IX:3, italics added.
37. Cunningham *Historical Theology*, vol. 1, 621, italics added.

receives the grace of justification, and that involves the twofold benefit of forgiveness of sin and adoption into the family of God.

We have seen that the results of Adam's fall involved his guilt and loss of original righteousness, the imputation of the guilt of his sin to his posterity (by ordinary generation), the transmission to them of a fallen nature, and the total depravity of the faculties of the soul, implying the bondage of the will or the loss of free will as to any action of spiritual good. The question arises, then, as it was put by Job of old: "[H]ow should "man be just with God?" (Job 9:1); or the puzzled response of the disciples of Christ recurs, "Who then can be saved?" Whatever the answer, reconciliation with God cannot in any respect turn on personal and individual merit or competence or worth. Reconciliation must of necessity rest entirely in the hands of God. Our entire argument of individual incapacity of soul points inevitably in that direction.

In the most straightforward of terms, to be "just" in the eyes of God means that one's relation to the law of God is what it ought to be. It is precisely the absence of that "justness" that characterizes the state of sin. The declaration of the gospel, therefore, is that God himself establishes the necessary state by placing to the sinner's account the righteousness of Christ. We confront again the fact that Christ came into the world to be the sinner's substitute in the twofold aspect of keeping the law of God perfectly on the sinner's behalf and in paying the penalty of sin to which all were exposed. The doctrine and fact of justification amount to the statement that God is "just, and the justifier of him which believeth in Jesus" (Rom 3:26) by reason that the covenant of grace that he established with his people in Christ culminated in that remarkable substitution. We look more closely, then, at the crucial issue of the imputation of righteousness that God thereby effects.

When we look to the substitutionary death of Christ we see that involved in it is what we may refer to as a reciprocal imputation. First, in order that Christ might bear the penalty of sin, there was imputed to him, or again placed by God to his account, the guilt of sin for which his atonement was made. By that action the sinner's guilt was imputed to Christ. But at that point the character of God's own justness would, on the face of it, stand in the way of the very action that was therein contemplated. For God, who cannot lie, cannot, consistent with his own rectitude, declare a thing to be that is not. As Turretin puts it, "God cannot show favor to, nor justify anyone without a perfect righteousness. For since the judgment of God is according to truth, he cannot pronounce anyone just who is not really just."[38] Similarly, God cannot declare one to be guilty who is not guilty. Therefore, in order to declare his Son to be guilty, in order that the punishment of sin and guilt might be laid upon him, it was necessary that he should first be *constituted* guilty. God effects that necessity and he constitutes his own Son guilty by imputing to him the sin of those for whom he is about to die. God thereby *constitutes* his Son guilty in order then to be able truthfully to *declare* him guilty.

By the same token, in order to be able truthfully to declare that the sinner is now just, or righteous, God gives to the sinner the forensic righteousness of Christ. By that act of imputing to the sinner that substitutionary righteousness, God *constitutes* him righteous in order then to be able truthfully to *declare* him righteous.[39] It is then that divine act of reciprocal imputation, the imputation of the sinner's sin to Christ and the imputation of Christ's righteousness to the sinner, that is encapsulated in the biblical doctrine of justification. Justification, then, is a once-for-all declarative, forensic statement of God that one who is not in himself just, or righteous, is now reconciled to God in a state of righteousness. That righteousness accrues on the grounds of the substitution that the messianic-redemptive mission and accomplishment of Christ involved.

But we have spoken throughout of the immediacy of God and of his actions in the interest of his eternal purpose of redemption. We have referred to the immediacy of God in his being and his knowledge, and to the immediacy of his imputation to Adam's posterity of the guilt of his sin. We are now able to state that the imputation of sin and righteousness that we have explored again involves actions of God's immediacy.

By immediacy we mean again the absence of any mediate or intervening secondary cause that stands between God's intention, design, and action and the result in human experience. As to the imputation of sin to Christ, it would be a mistake of unimaginable order to assume that any mediating cause stood between the dictates of God's will and the effectuation of that will in the substitutionary punishment of his Son who died

---

38. Turretin, *Institutes*, vol. 2, 647.

39. See the very valuable discussion of the imputation of sin and righteousness that is involved in God's statement of justification in Murray, *Epistle to the Romans*, vol. 1, 178–210.

for us in his human nature. The reality is that God's action was dictated by his sovereign will as that was informed by his love for those he gave to his Son to redeem. We have no recourse to explanation more ultimate than the will of God. "He loved us," the apostle John said, "and sent his Son to be the propitiation for our sins" (1 John 4:10).

It is true that Christ's perfect obedience in his human nature to the law of God qualified him to discharge the office of priest on our behalf by dying for sin. But as we shall see in a subsequent chapter in Part Two below, the obedience in view was made by a human nature that was not only sinless but was impeccable, or, that is, was incapable of sin. Because Christ was, at the point of his substitutionary death, free of sin on his own account for which punishment could be due, he was qualified to carry and pay the penalty for the sin of others. But the point precisely at issue at this stage is that God the Father, in laying the penalty of sin upon his Son, was acting in a manner that was constrained only by his own will. That will had been completely specified in what we have seen as the predeterminate council of the Godhead before the foundation of the world.

When, at the same time, we contemplate the imputation to the sinner of Christ's righteousness, the righteousness of Christ in both his keeping the law and his dying in response to the demands of the law, we recognize again a divine act of immediate imputation. For if that were not so, the question would arise as to what might be the mediating cause that stood between God's intention and act on the one hand and the sinner's constitution in righteousness on the other. But our preceding argument amounts to the effect that the individual who, until the grace of God comes to him, is bound in sin, has no ability at all to make any contribution to his own rescue from that state and condition. It might be rejoined by arguments from, for example, the Arminian perspective that when the divine call to belief in Christ comes to the individual with the offer of salvation he is free to accept or reject it. But any such suggestion is destroyed by what has been said of the state of sin, the disabilities that sin has imposed on the faculties of the soul, and the consequent bondage of the will and its incapacity as to anything of spiritual value. It would again be a mistake of the highest order to imagine, in the sense of the Arminian perspective, that the faith of the sinner at the point of justification constitutes a mediating cause of the imputation to him of the righteousness of Christ. For that very faith, it has been seen, is itself the gift of God that accrues to the sinner in the Holy Spirit's conveyance to him of the grace of regeneration.

There is no escape, in reality or in doctrinal formation, from the fact that the sinner's salvation is, in all its parts, the sovereign effect of the grace of God.

It is true again that the faith by which the sinner reaches out to Christ and relies on him in repentance and trust is the instrument by which he is brought to the point of justification. But the faith he exercises, the gift of God by grace, is in no sense a meritorious cause of his salvation. It is, as has just been said, an instrumental cause, and the meritorious cause of salvation rests in the Person of Christ and his substitutionary work on the sinner's behalf. Both the instrumental and the meritorious cause trace back to the efficacious cause of salvation in the sovereign will and grace of God.

We are left with the conclusion that as the imputation of the guilt of Adam's sin to his posterity is an *immediate imputation*, so the imputation of Christ's righteousness to the sinner is again an *immediate imputation*.

When we say that the entrance to life eternal begins at the point of the conveyance to the soul of the grace of regeneration that issues in saving faith in Christ and God's declarative statement of justification, we say also that that is the beginning of the Christian journey. Ahead lies the on-going ministry to the soul of the Holy Spirit in his work of sanctification. We turn to consider that divine work in the next chapter, and it will be seen that again important aspects of immediacy are involved, as well as action on the part of the person who has now been renewed in soulish state.

5

Immediacy in Sanctification

THE APOSTLE PAUL STRUCK to the heart of the meaning and possibility of Christian sanctification when he declared that by the action of God Christ is made unto the those who believe in him wisdom, righteousness, sanctification, and redemption (1 Cor 1:30). The recognition of the messianic-redemptive commission of Christ is incomplete until the benefits that accrue from his obedience and atonement project their significance to the Christian life. Those benefits include the declaration of justification and reconciliation with God, adoption into the family of God or incorporation into the kingdom of Christ, and, as we shall now consider it, progress in sanctification.

Justification, it is to be said, is prior to sanctification in the sense of what is now in view as progressive development in holiness. God by his Spirit ministers the grace of sanctification to those who have been established in a state of justification.[1] But the definitive, declarative statement of justification, whereby God accepts the sinner as righteous in his sight, is not itself an action that makes the individual beneficiary of it holy. Justification is a forensic statement of God. It has to do with one's relation to law. Whereas the sinner was previously under the condemnation of the law of God, now, by reason of the imputation to him of the righteousness of Christ, his standing in relation to the law is entirely different. "In due time Christ died," it is declared, "for the ungodly" (Rom 5:6). The individual who was once ungodly, unjust, in that his relation to the law was not what it should have been, is now regarded as godly by virtue of the righteousness of Christ that has been given to him. But while justification is thus a definitive, once-for-all, and totally forensic statement, more is to

---

1. See VanDrunen, "The Two Kingdoms," 207.

be said of the sinner's new status. We have already seen the nature of the benefits conveyed to the individual in the grace of regeneration. We have been alerted to what Murray refers to the "decisive action that occurs at the inception of the Christian life ... that characterizes the people of God in their identity as called effectually by God's grace."[2] In the complex of the conveyance of the grace of regeneration, in the communication of new life, in the transference "from the power of darkness ... into the kingdom of [God's] dear Son" (Col 1:13) and the effective translation thereby from wrath to grace, one is established in a new state of holiness. At that point, and within that complex of grace, an existential union with Christ and a sealing as a redeemed child of God have been established. The new state of holiness in which the beneficiary of grace now stands is what is referred to as the individual's definitive sanctification. He is now holy in the sight of God.

We reflect on what we have already contemplated as the divine covenant of redemption that issued from the predeterminate council of the Godhead, and we recall the distribution of redemptive offices among the triune Persons, the Father, the Son, and the Holy Spirit. It was the declared and assigned office of the Holy Spirit to apply to those for whom Christ died the benefits of the redemption he accomplished and to conduct them to glory. The nature of the Spirit's action to that effect will be examined in what follows. But the Pauline statement to the Corinthians says that it is Christ who is the Christian's sanctification. That attribution to Christ is necessary and meaningful in two respects. First, it is the completion of the messianic-redemptive work of Christ that forms the basis of, or that provides the divinely accepted warrant for, the Holy Spirit's work of sanctification. Second, when the relation between the work of Christ and that of the Spirit is seen in the form in which Christ himself stated it, it is clear that it is Christ himself who is furthering the Christian's sanctification through his Spirit. For in his discourse to his disciples on the night on which he was betrayed he had given them the promise and explanation that "when he, the Spirit of truth, is come, he will guide you into all truth: for he shall not speak of himself; but whatsoever he shall hear, that shall he speak.... He shall glorify me: for he shall receive of mine, and show it unto you" (John 16:13–14).

---

2. Murray, *Collected Writings*, vol. 2, 278.

By sanctification, then, is meant the unique place (definitive sanctification) and the distinctive quality of life (progressive sanctification) that is attributable to the Christian person in his life in this world. The root meaning of the word implies that by reason of the regenerating grace of God and the justification in which it issues, the individual who is the beneficiary of it is thereby set apart for God in an entirely new relationship. By the definitive transference that is thereby effected, the person who was once the slave of the devil (John 8:44) is now enslaved to Christ. He is now the property of Christ, "bought with a price" (1 Cor 6:20), redeemed "with the precious blood of Christ" (1 Pet 1:19), and he now finds himself devoted to the cause of Christ. The transference from the kingdom of Satan (Eph 2:2) to the kingdom of Christ is made once-for-all, it is definitive and indissoluble, and it holds the promise of eternal security and benefit.

That establishment of the believer in a new relationship within the kingdom of Christ we have referred to as "definitive sanctification."[3] The believer is thereby set apart for God. The transference involved is the immediate work of God and it involves as an essential element the implantation within the soul of a new *habitus* or disposition or principle of action that is an endowment of the Spirit's work of regeneration. In that statement we again have in view, as in earlier argument, the *immediacy* of God's salvific action, meaning by that that no element of *mediacy*, no mediating instrument or cause, intervened between God's action directed to the outcome and the realization of it. Again, in the initial sanctification of the believer in Christ, no explanatory principle or mediating event is relevant other than God's action in accordance with the dictates of his own will. God acts sovereignly in accordance with his will.

Within the complex of events related to and surrounding the outcome envisaged there are, it is true, certain responsive actions of the individual person, for example his response in belief, repentance, and faith to the call of Christ. But that response, it has already been seen, is itself the exercise of endowments of soul that have been conveyed to it by the *immediate* prior action of the Spirit of God. The abilities of soul that are thereby exercised are themselves the result of the *immediate* regenerating work of God by his Spirit. There is, of course, a time dimension involved in the exercise of the faith with which the individual has been endowed. In that connection Berkhof has drawn attention to the "reciprocal action"

---

3. See Murray, "Definitive Sanctification" in *Collected Writings*, vol. 2, 277.

that is involved at those points. "The initial act is that of Christ, who unites believers to himself by regenerating them and thus producing faith in them. On the other hand, the believer also unites himself to Christ by a conscious act of faith, and continues the union, under the influence of the Holy Spirit, by the constant exercise of faith."[4] Berkhof has here emphasized the distinction between the *endowment* of faith on the one hand, and the subsequent *exercise* of faith on the other.[5] The *endowment* of faith is the *immediate* work of the Spirit of God that occurs at a point in time. The *exercise* of faith, or the activation of the newly endowed capacity of faith, occurs in time and may be characterized by any of several time dimensions. Murray observes in relation to those actions that "regeneration pushes itself into consciousness and expresses itself in the exercises of faith and repentance."[6] But as to regeneration itself and the implications of it, Murray refers to regeneration as that act "of which faith and repentance are the *immediate* effects in our consciousness."[7] In that statement we may see the implication of *immediacy* in time in the endowment of faith and the *immediacy* of God's action in the sense of the absence of any mediating cause or influence.

PROGRESSIVE SANCTIFICATION

It was said in contemplating the work of the Holy Spirit that it incorporated both the conveyance to the Christian believer of the gifts and benefits that Christ purchased for him in his act of redemption and the conduct of the believer to glory. It is that last mentioned aspect of the work of the Holy Spirit to which we now turn.

The redemptive work of God comes to consummation in the life of the individual by his deliverance from the guilt, the power, and the pollution of sin. The deliverance from guilt we have inspected under the heading of the justifying act of God, in the reciprocal imputation of the sinner's guilt to Christ and the imputation of Christ's righteousness to the sinner. But it remains to be said that sin, that is actions of sin and even a principle of sin that wars against the soul, clings to the individual

---

4. Berkhof, *Systematic Theology*, 450.
5. We shall return to that distinction in a later chapter when the implications of the believer's union with Christ are considered.
6. Murray, *Collected Writings*, vol. 2, 198.
7. Ibid., 115, italics added.

throughout his life in this world. It is the office of the Holy Spirit, then, to bring his divine influence to bear on the consciousness and life of the individual in such a way that the power of sin is progressively destroyed and the soul progressively cleansed from the pollution of sin. That work of God in the soul takes up what is now referred to as progressive sanctification, to which definitive sanctification is the necessary antecedent.[8]

The Scriptural datum is to the effect that it is God who sanctifies (1 Thess 5:23). It is the work of God by and through the agency of his Spirit. Taking cognizance of the remaining "indwelling sin" (Rom 7:17) in the believer, the objective of the Spirit's ministry is the elimination of sin and its expression in the believer's life and the complete conformation of the believer to the image of Christ. That objective will not be fully realized until, as the letter to the Corinthians states, "this corruptible shall have put on incorruption, and this mortal shall have put on immortality" (1 Cor 15:54). With that final perspective in view, the author of the letter to the Hebrews reminds us of "holiness, without which no man shall see the Lord" (Heb 12:14). The reality of the human condition and prospect is "No holiness, no heaven."[9] What are the ways, then, in which the Spirit of God accomplishes those redemptive objectives of progressive sanctification to which he is committed?

The Spirit's operations in sanctification are encompassed in mystery. Mystery exists, that is to say, for us who are confined in the finitude of our createdness, while no mystery exists for God who before the foundation of the world ordained all things that come to pass. When it is said that God "worketh all things after the counsel of his own will" (Eph 1:11), included in the "all things" are the foreseen and ordered operations of his Spirit in what we are now considering as his work of sanctification. But while it is necessary to make further observations on the mystery that exists in the Spirit's operations, it must at the same time be recognized that in the process of his sanctification the believer is not entirely passive. There is decidedly an active element in his sanctification, an element for which he is positively responsible.

That can be put alternatively in the manner of Paul's statement to the Philippian church. "[W]ork out your own salvation with fear and trembling. For it is God which worketh in you both to will and to do of his

---

8. See Murray, *Collected Writings*, vol. 2, 294 on "Progressive Sanctification."
9. Alderson, *No Holiness, No Heaven*.

good pleasure" (Phil 2:12–13). Involved in that statement is not simply that God gives to the individual the power to do what he is obliged to do for the furtherance of his sanctification. That God does so is, of course, true. But at stake in the statement also is the fact that God will do in and for the individual all that he has purposed to do for that person's progress toward conformity to the image of Christ. Coming to focus, therefore, is the sovereignty of God in the individual's sanctification. That datum will be ignored to the peril of the believer's understanding of his status and prospects. It forces the conclusion, moreover, that just as we hold that it is the Holy Spirit of God who is the *agent* of the Godhead in the process of sanctification, so we hold also to the *sovereignty* of the Spirit in that operation. We shall return to the point.

But recognizing the responsibility that lies on the individual for his progress in sanctification, two things are to be said. First, the sharpest possible differentiation arises at this point between the believer's regeneration and his sanctification. For in the former the individual is necessarily passive and has no part to play in his regeneration which is a secret, sovereign, and unsolicited work of the Holy Spirit within the soul.[10] Now however, as a result of that regeneration, the individual to whom the renewing grace of God has been conveyed by the Spirit is no longer dead. He is now very much alive, alive, that is, to the things of God and to consequent spiritual realities. Secondly, therefore, being now alive unto God, the individual is able to act, he is responsible to act, and he has a decided part to play in his sanctification. The difference in the two instances implies that in God's act of justification that follows from the precedent regeneration, the righteousness of Christ is *imputed* to the sinner. Now that his sanctification is in progress, the righteousness of Christ is progressively *imparted* to him. In accomplishing that, there comes to effect a joint activity of the believer and the Spirit of God.

It would be a mistake of the highest order to conclude, however, that any contradiction exists in that connection between what Bavinck rightly refers to as the "all-encompassing activity of God in grace and the self-agency of people maintained alongside of it."[11] But before the reasons for the lack of contradiction are explored further, light can be thrown on the possibilities that exist by taking note of the individual's responsibilities in

---

10. See the discussion of regeneration in the preceding chapter,
11. Bavinck, *Reformed Dogmatics: Volume 4*, 254.

sanctification. Two things are involved: first, an increasing sensitivity on the part of the individual to the presence and the sinfulness of sin; and second, the manner of dealing with sin that comes to life in the individual and with the disposition and proclivity to sin that remains within the soul.

It is part of the ministry of the Holy Spirit to raise the sensitivities of the soul progressively to the meaning of sin.[12] The sin involved is not confined to overt actions, but also to what the Psalmist referred to as his "secret faults" (Ps 19:12). By that is meant not only sins that are secret in the sense that they might be successfully hidden from public observation or from the knowledge of the church, but sins which are secret in the sense that the individual himself might not be consciously aware of them. Such is the rigor of the mandate, "Be ye holy," God says, "for I am holy" (1 Pet 1:16; Lev 11:44). The remark of the Puritans is cogent, that it is the most advanced saint who is most conscious of the sinfulness of sin.

The part to be played by the individual Christian in the process of his sanctification is referred to as the mortification of sin. That means putting to death, by the grace of God, the unruly motions within the soul that lead to sin. Paul presented to the Colossian church an argument that combined in concise fashion the doctrine of the true believers' position in Christ and the ethical imperatives that followed as a result. By reason that they were "risen with Christ," the imperative upon them was to "Set your affections on things above, not on things of the earth" (Col 3:1–2). Further, and in the light of that, "Mortify therefore your members which are upon the earth," (Col 3:5); and the same apostle argued to the Romans, "[B]rethren, we are debtors, not to the flesh, to live after the flesh. For if ye live after the flesh, ye shall die: but if ye *through the Spirit* do mortify the deeds of the body, ye shall live" (Rom 8:12–13, italics added). The argument is as insistent as it is relevant to the individual's part in his own sanctification. "What shall we say then? Shall we continue in sin, that grace may abound? God forbid. How shall we, that are dead to sin, live any longer therein? . . . Let not sin therefore reign in your mortal body, that ye should obey it in the lusts thereof" (Rom 6:1–2, 12). The Scriptural data could be multiplied. In summary, and looking at the individual's responsibility in

---

12. In that connection an extensive and highly valuable literature exists which cannot be explored at this point. See, for example, Venning, *The Plague of Plagues*; three treatises by Owen, *On the Mortification of Sin*; *On Temptation*; and *On Indwelling Sin in Believers*, in *Works of John Owen*, vol. 6; Bavinck, *Reformed Dogmatics: Volume 3*, 25–190.

this matter, the conclusion follows that there will be no progress in sanctification unless and until there is progress in the mortification of sin.

FREE WILL AND THE SOVEREIGNTY OF THE SPIRIT

The second question to be confronted in this connection has to do with what Bavinck referred to as the "self-agency" of the person who is the subject of the Holy Spirit's work of progressive sanctification. We addressed at some length in the preceding chapter the meaning to be attached to the claim of human free will. The question returns in sharpened significance as we hold in view again what we have now observed as the sovereignty of the Holy Spirit in sanctification and the responsibility of the individual.

It was argued at an earlier stage that it is necessary to hold to the *immediacy* of God in his being, his knowledge, and his will, and to the claim that God is sovereign in all his purposes, objectives, and ordinations. If that conclusion is to be held, then the short answer to any claims to the contrary at this point is to insist again that God the Holy Spirit is sovereign in all his works, including now his works of sanctification. That, in shortest compass, establishes the *immediacy* of God the Spirit in the believer's sanctification. By that we mean that if, as is demonstrably true on the basis of adequate Scriptural data, God by his Spirit will accomplish all that he has purposed with reference to the believer's redemption, then no mediating event or cause stands between the operation of the Spirit and the outcome that is aimed at in the Christian's sanctification. Again that is not saying that the Christian is passive throughout the process of his sanctification and that he does nothing. What is being said is that the sovereign operations of the Spirit are, as has been said, mysterious. It is not possible for us to resolve all elements of mystery at this crucial point. But certain observations in relation to them can be made.

In another aspect we are confronted again at this point with what is to be said of the sovereign providence of God. And in that connection again, what is to be said of the status of man who, by creation fiat, is the property of God? We have said that because all of created reality that God spoke into existence is the property of God, he retains complete rights of disposal over all that he has made. We have seen that as to his initial endowment of free will man made use of that to repudiate his covenantal obligations to God. And while mystery exists as to God's endowment of our first parents with the prerogatives of free will, the Scriptural data that declare the fact are clear. We bow before them as conveying to us the speech of God. We concur with the summary of à Brakel: "In our discussion of *free will* it should be noted first of all that man's free will is not independent from God. Man is totally dependent upon God in regard (1) to his being, (2) to his activity, (3) to God's prerogative to obligate him to His will and laws . . . and (4) to the foreknowledge and decree of God, for he infallibly knows *and has decreed* that every matter and deed will have a certain outcome and none other."[13]

In all his works the Holy Spirit acts according to the will of the Godhead in the matter of the providential ordering of the history of reality and, in particular in the present instance, the accomplishment of the objective of applying to those for whom Christ died the full benefits of his redemption. That includes, notably, the progressive conformation of those individuals to the image of Christ and the presentation of them to Christ at the last day. But let us sharpen the focus of thought further.

If, as has just been stated, God in the Person of his Spirit is sovereign in and over all the affairs of men, does that sovereignty extend to *all* of the *actions* of men? We answer in the affirmative. Further, does that sovereignty extend to all the *thoughts* of men? We again answer in the affirmative. In other words, the all-comprehending sovereignty of God requires it to be said that it is not possible for any individual to *do* anything that God has not ordained. It is not possible for man to do anything that God has not already thought. But further, our claim, then, is that it is correspondingly not possible for any individual to *think* anything that God has not already thought. "I know the thoughts that come into your mind," God has said, "every one of them" (Ezek 11:5). He knows the thought because he ordained the thought. "The lot is cast into the lap; but the whole disposing thereof is of the Lord" (Prov 16:33). "The king's heart is in the hand of the Lord, as the rivers of water: he turneth it whithersoever he will" (Prov 21:1). It would be inadequate to say that the Spirit orders only the external events and experiences in the life of the individual he is committed to bring to glory. The Spirit moves in the innermost recesses of the soul. He thinks the thoughts of holiness in us, and he thereby structures our lives and our progress.

It is not necessary to repeat in detail for its relevance at this point that the human will does not function independently of the intellect. Edwards'

---

13. à Brakel, *The Christian's Reasonable Service*, vol. 1, 407–8, italics added.

treatise on the will established the point once and for all. So that while the will is free from outside compulsion, and while an individual cannot be forced to do something he does not will to do, nevertheless it is necessarily subject to both the internal faculties of the soul in the manner we have seen, and, it is now being said, to the mysterious supervision and direction of the will of God. For in the will of God, and under the control of the sovereign ordering of God, all of the forces of history and the formation of character that bear on the formation and functioning of an individual's faculties transmit their effects, impulses, and determinations to the will and its actions. The freedom of the will can be said, then, to be one of "necessary consequence," to use à Brakel's felicitous phrase.[14] In the same sense, the argument of Jonathan Edwards' *Freedom of the Will* establishes him as a necessitarian. But it is important to note that in the case of both Edwards and à Brakel their necessitarianism rests within the orbit of, and is subject to, the all-comprehending ordination and will of God. That is the nature of the theological genius of their work. The will is necessarily subject to the determinative forces we have indicated, the internal capacities of the soul and God's providential ordering of all things.

The significance of what has been said for the individual believer's progress in sanctification is clear. God works, and man works. But that working of God and man does not amount to a synergism such as we rejected when we spoke of man's justification and reconciliation with God. In that case there was not, and there could not have been, any possibility of synergism because at the time of the coming of the renewing grace of God the individual is "dead in trespasses and sins" (Eph 2:1). We do not need to repeat the details of the argument and claim. In the present case of progress in sanctification, the working of the Christian person in the discharge of his ethical responsibilities that point to his sanctification is, as has now been said, decidedly under the supervision, direction, and support of the Holy Spirit.

The relations we have in view may be clarified further by recalling what regeneration has been seen to involve. We can say, to use the words of Dabney, that "it *reverses* the moral *habitus* [i.e., disposition] of the believer's will, prevalently [that is, a new disposition is prevalent, or prevails, in the soul], but not at first absolutely, and that the work of progressive sanctification carries on this change, thus omnipotently begun, towards

---

14. à Brakel, op. cit., 409–10.

that absolute completeness which we must possess on entering heaven. In the carnal state the *habitus* of the sinner's will is absolutely and exclusively godless. In the regenerate state it is prevalently but not completely godly. In the glorified state it is absolutely and exclusively godly."[15]

The progressive sanctification of the Christian person is to be set, then, against the continuation of sin in the person. In Dabney's perfectly proper conception, it is the work of the Holy Spirit in the soul gradually and progressively to conform the *habitus* (disposition) within the will to the requirements of holiness that the Christian's new estate mandates. It is therefore a part of the Christian life and experience that as the sanctifying work of the Spirit of God in the soul progresses, the individual becomes progressively aware of the meaning of sin. But now that we face the reality of sin, how is that to be explained in the person who is characterized by a wholly different nature? The old *habitus* resides in the person, the old principle of action that can and does at times pull the believer into occasions of sin. It is simply that old habits, old preferences, and old alignments can and do from time to time raise their head and remind the believer of the old pleasures of sin. For that reason, sin in the life of the believer is explained, first, by the pressures and temptations to sin that come from outside of himself; and secondly, by the capacity to respond to that by the habits of earlier life whose ingrained residence in the soul is being progressively displaced.

It is apposite to note that the same conclusions have been stated in different terms by the seventeenth-century Puritan theologian, John Owen. In his treatise, *A Discourse Concerning the Holy Spirit*, Owen addresses the reality of sin in the life of the regenerate person. "One thing yet remains to be cleared," Owen says, "that there may be no mistake in this matter; and this is, that in those who are thus constantly inclined and disposed unto all the acts of a heavenly, spiritual life, there are yet remaining contrary dispositions and inclinations also. There are yet in them inclinations and dispositions to sin, *proceeding from the remainders of a contrary habitual principle* .... This yet continueth in them, inclining them unto evil and all that is so, according to the power and efficacy that is remaining unto it in various degrees."[16] The remaining ability to be led astray into sin by old habits and imaginations has been referred to in

---

15. Dabney, *Discussions*, vol. 1, 196–97.
16. Owen, *Discourse Concerning the Holy Spirit*, in *Works*, vol. 3, 488, italics added.

doctrinal terms as "indwelling sin," of which Paul wrote eloquently in the seventh chapter of his letter to the Romans.

But the sovereign administration to the soul by the Holy Spirit continues. He steps into the Christian's experience and, as John Owen puts it, "he . . . stops the course of sin." Observe how Owen makes the point. "When lust hath conceived, and is ready to bring forth—when the soul lies at the brink of some iniquity—he [God] gives in seasonable help, relief, deliverance, and safety. Here lies a great part of the care and faithfulness of Christ towards his poor saints. He will not suffer them to be worried with the power of sin, nor to be carried out unto ways that shall dishonour the gospel, or fill them with shame and reproach, and so render them useless in the world; but he steps in with the saving relief and assistance of his grace, *stops the course of sin*, and makes them in himself more than conquerors. And this assistance lies under the promise, 1 Cor 10:13."[17]

It is true that in his ministry to the soul the Holy Spirit "moves in a mysterious way."[18] The hymn writer, Harriet Auber, has captured the meaning of what is involved in her conclusion that "Every thought of holiness [is] his alone."[19] The Holy Spirit, in the discharge of his redemptive assignment, is thus vitally active in the Christian believer's progress in sanctification. The apostolic conclusion, therefore, arrests us: "[H]e which hath begun a good work in you will perform it until the day of Jesus Christ" (Phil 1:6).

A final point remains. Let it be said that the Holy Spirit is, in the ways we have seen, sovereignly active in furthering the Christian believer's sanctification, and let it be acknowledged that in his exercise of the will of God for the salvation of his people the Spirit acts with an immediacy that characterizes the actions of the Godhead. Let it be said that the Spirit will and does influence the activation of means to the ends to which he is committed, by motivating, for example, the Christian's own actions in the mortification of sin and the use of the means of grace that further sanctification. Let it be said also that the end and objective of the Spirit's

---

17. Owen, "The Nature and Power of Indwelling Sin," in *Works*, vol. 6, 277, italics added. The preceding four paragraphs are heavily dependent on argument in Vickers, *Texture of Truth*, 150–58.

18. Cowper, *God moves in a mysterious way his wonders to perform*, in Trinity Hymnal, 128.

19. Auber, *Our blest Redeemer, ere He breathed His tender, last farewell*, in Congregational Praise, 209.

purpose, the presentation of the redeemed host in the last great day in perfect holiness and in perfect conformation at last to the image of Christ, cannot fail of achievement. But what is to be said of the possibilities envisaged in those several projections if, in fact, the Christian believer fails to play his part in sanctification's processes? Is it really possible, then, that the entire cause might be lost?

To answer such a question in the affirmative would be to deny and to controvert all that has been said to this point regarding the sovereignty of the Spirit of God in the design and realization of the objectives to which he is committed. Further, such a conclusion would overlook entirely the means by which God in himself has not only guaranteed the end of perfect redemption but does, in fact, bring it about. For as the argument of the apostle in the twelfth chapter of the letter to the Hebrews makes clear, the divine discipline that God exercises with regard to his people is effective to the ends envisaged. No longer does the Christian stand in the position of Adam, where failure to obey would result in the loss of righteousness and the original estate of godliness and would result in the agony of looming perdition. It was possible for Adam not to sin, *posse non peccare*, but in the condition of mutability in which he was established it was possible for him to fall. But now the Christian's position is vastly different from that which our first parents enjoyed. Now the Christian's position is not only *posse non peccare*, but one of *non posse peccare*, not possible to sin, or, that is, not possible to fall away and be eternally lost.

By that last statement it is meant that it is not now possible for the Christian to fall from the estate to which he has been raised by virtue of the union with Christ in which he has been established by the regenerating grace of God. The apostle was eloquent on the point when he said to the Romans, "But where sin abounded, grace did much more abound" (Rom 5:20). Sin abounded in Adam's fall. But the truth in Paul's statement that grace more abounded is that by the grace of God the individual is raised, not simply to the state and condition that Adam occupied before he fell, but to a much higher state. That higher state is that he is now joined to Christ in a vital, spiritual, and indissoluble union. Adam was not in that existential respect joined to Christ. He would have realized the corresponding benefits of confirmation in holiness and likeness to God and eternal felicity if he had not sinned. But now, by reason of the union with Christ that he enjoys, and unlike Adam, the Christian believer can never fall from his union with Christ.

But we have seen that the Christian sins. We do not minimize the fact. But when the apostle John said that "Whosoever is born of God doth not commit sin . . . and he cannot sin, because he is born of God" (1 John 3:9), he was saying that it is impossible for the Christian to consent to continue in sin. Why, again, should that be so? The answer, so far as it turns on the sovereign ministry of the Spirit of God, is twofold.

First, it is the office and function of the Holy Spirit to convey to the Christian soul the conviction of sin or, as we have seen, a progressive awareness and sensitivity to the meaning of sin. The Christian as he grows in the grace of God is increasingly afraid of sin. He flees from it. Second, it is a highly significant reality in the Christian life that God uses the means of his disciplinary grace to rescue the Christian from sin and to direct his people back to the paths of righteousness. "My son," the writer to the Hebrews says, "despise not thou the chastening of the Lord, nor faint when thou art rebuked of him: For whom the Lord loveth he chasteneth, and scourgeth every son whom he receiveth" (Heb 12:5–6).

"Beloved," John says, "now are we the sons of God, and it doth not yet appear what we shall be: but we know that, when he shall appear, we shall be like him; for we shall see him as he is" (1 John 3:2). That is the end to which, not only is the Holy Spirit committed in his ministry to the soul, but to which, as a result, the Christian will arrive at the completion of his progressive sanctification.

Part Two
Applications

Introduction to Part Two

The intent of the three chapters in this Part is to explore more fully the applications to the Christian life of the doctrinal conclusions that have now been established. Two objectives are in view. First, several of the previously stated doctrines will be restated and recalled in new or expanded form and explored further as their application is considered. The overlap with previous discussions in a few instances is intentional in order to permit reading of what follows independently of previous argument. Second, by bringing the relation between doctrine and application into closer scrutiny it is hopefully possible to disabuse the Christian mind of a fallacy that seems to have acquired wider currency than it deserves. That is the mistake of imagining that a conceptual separation between doctrine and application is desirable or can be effected in the postmodern intellectual climate, or that a tension necessarily exists between them.

Biblical doctrine is not completely or sufficiently well apprehended until its applications in practice are explored and understood. The former without the latter is in danger of descending to a mere, and, it might be said, an empty and purposeless intellectualism. Application without doctrine, on the other hand, threatens to become nothing more than mere human psychology. There can be application in the Christian life only when there is doctrine to be applied.

The first chapter of this Part addresses the relation between the Christian mind and the mind of Christ and draws on what has already been said regarding the analogical relation that the individual's knowledge bears to the knowledge of God. The proposition that underlies the argument is that Christianity is a highly rational religion. That is to say, the intellectual faculty of the soul is deeply and actively engaged in it; not, it will be recalled from previous discussion, reason in its unregenerate state, but reason as renewed in its capacities by the grace of regeneration. To say that the Christian faith is entirely rational is in no sense to embrace a rational*ism*.

The second chapter endeavors to bring to prominence a clearer meaning of the redemptive work of Christ, with particular reference to his atonement and resurrection, than certain contemporary theologies contemplate. The chapter recalls what has been said of the Person of Christ and reflects on his impeccability in this world or, that is, on the impossibility that he could sin. What Christ did and achieved in his redemptive work accrued, not to what has been argued in some contemporary theologies as his own justification, but to the justification of those for whose benefit his redemptive mission was instituted.

The final chapter speaks to the tensions that exist in the practice of the Christian life, notwithstanding the Christian person's indissoluble adoption into the family of God. It raises from a Christian theological perspective issues of both epistemology (what and how can a Christian know) and soteriology (what is the meaning of salvation) and brings to bear on them the truth that both the epistemological and the soteriological problems are resolved in Christ in whom are hid all the treasures of wisdom and knowledge.

6

The Christian Mind and the Mind of Christ

IN THE OPENING CHAPTERS of his first letter to the Corinthians the apostle Paul provided an extended exposure of the ignorance, foolishness, and futility of non-Christian thought. The details will be familiar. The natural man, he concluded, did not and could not understand the realities of the Christian revelation. That was because, first, those realities were spiritually discerned, and second, the natural mind was darkened by reason of its participation in the bequest of Adam's fall. As a result of the fall a terrible inability attached to the human cognitive capacity (1 Cor 2:14). But Paul's argument culminated in an astonishing statement that challenges our understanding of the Christian's status and condition. The Christian, Paul says, has the mind of Christ (1 Cor 2:16).

The present discussion is motivated by the apostle's conclusion. It brings into focus a number of implications and considerations that bear on the Christian's identity and his prospects both for this life and for that which is to come. It is not necessary to labor the point that we confront at this time a deeper theological confusion, along with an accelerating doctrinal deviation from what Reformation theology has been and has meant, than have previously disturbed the church. If the biblical doctrine is to be preserved and its meaning and impact sustained, it has become urgently necessary to hold a clearer understanding of who the Christian man is, what it is that describes the high status to which he has been raised by reason of his union with Christ, and what it is that determines his ethic and his life in the everyday. We are pointed, thereby, to the threefold question of the Christian's being, his knowledge, and his behavior. In other terms, we want to understand from a biblical perspective the Christian believer's true identity and being, what it is he knows and how that knowledge is securely established, and what, in the light of that, is the ethic by which he lives. In more technical terms, we are challenged by the realities of a

Christian ontology, a Christian epistemology, and a Christian ethics. I put the issue in those terms because of the deeper doctrinal significance of the relation that properly exists between those categories. Let me observe, first, on what that involves.

Immanuel Kant, the philosopher in whose work the eighteenth-century Enlightenment culminated, gave to the world of thought his so-called Copernican revolution in epistemology that effectively determined the death of metaphysics or ontology. We need to take that achievement and its results seriously and carefully because of the manner in which its influence has tarnished theology and, in more recent times, has shifted the church away from its Reformation commitment. What Kant did was to bring to prominence the question of knowledge, of what and how we know, and to make the answer rely on what can only be called the autonomy of the human intellect and its innate capacity. For Kant, and for the positivism to which his work gave birth in the nineteenth century, knowledge was possible only of things in the world of experience, things that could be seen and touched and handled and subject to empirical test. In fact, knowledge of those things depended, in turn, on the exercise of certain so-called categories within the autonomous mind that interpreted and in effect established the factness of what was observed and therefore knowable. The upshot of that development was that the human mind did not simply observe and know the brute facts of experience, but it operated in such a way as to establish the facticity of the facts by its own sovereign interpretative construction. The details can be observed in the literature on the history of thought and I have adverted to them in other places.[1]

In Kantian terms and in accordance with his extreme empiricism, knowledge was possible only of what was contained in the so-called phenomenal realm. But behind the phenomenal appearances and occurrences there was the "thing in itself," the *ding an sich*, which was unknowable. That existed in the so-called noumenal as distinct from the phenomenal realm. The importance of that for our present purposes is that Kant consigned God to the noumenal realm in which, as has just been said, knowledge was not possible. It is important to observe that while Kant, in that single philosophic wave of the hand, made God unknowable, his conclusion was that God may or may not exist; we simply did not know and could not know. In fairness, while Kant argued that it was impossible to "prove" the existence

---

1. See Vickers, *When God Converts a Sinner*, 52–54.

of God, it was equally impossible, he said, to prove that God did not exist. It was, for certain purposes, adequate to proceed "as if" God existed.

When we say, contrary to Kant and the bequest he has made to modern theology, that it is possible to know God, or when we say as Paul has done that "we have the mind of Christ," we are turning modern philosophy and the thought-system of the world on its head. We have seen that the latter day focus on epistemology, on the question of knowledge and knowing, has meant the death of ontology or the question of being. Indeed, it is cogently arguable that contemporary postmodernism has collapsed thought into an agnosticism in which being and knowledge are both surrendered. But that is another question outside our present interest.[2] Our argument, to the contrary, is simply that being is prior to knowing, that ontology is prior to epistemology. By that we mean that the "what" of knowledge is prior to the "how" of knowledge. What there is to be known determines the very possibility and process of knowledge itself.[3] For in the same way as our basic apologetic presupposition is that *God is*, our entire understanding of the Christian's position and prospects is what it is because God has spoken and, moreover, has established a redemption for sinners who were lost in the darkened grip of ignorance and rebellion against him. Further, we hold that the very possibility of human knowledge follows from the fact that God has creatively established the truth criteria, as well as the processes of validity, of knowledge. We say that man exists and thinks because God exists and thinks. Man speaks because God speaks. Man knows what he knows derivatively because what he knows and can know is analogical of the fullness of knowledge contained in God. God created all things out of nothing. Or we may say that God spoke all things *into* nothing. The definitive proof of the existence of God is that if God had not first spoken there would be no possibility at all of human thought or action. Indeed it has been rightly said that in order to deny that God exists one must stand on the ground that God has established. That is the final irony of agnosticism.

What is at issue, then, is the status and capacities of the Christian individual as determined by what the eternally existing God has said and done. The deepest reality that is implied, the fact that illumines our aware-

---

2. See the discussion in Vickers, *Fracture of Faith*, 160–62, and the same author's *Christian Confession*, 34–36.

3. Van Til, in his presuppositionalist apologetic and epistemology, has eloquently made the point. See his *Defense of the Faith*, chapters 2–4.

ness on the level we are now addressing, is that by reason of a sovereign, regenerating work of God's Holy Spirit, "we have the mind of Christ." We shall work out the meaning of what is involved in the following stages. First, we shall note some aspects of what revelation has said regarding the Christian mind and the mind of Christ; second, it will be necessary to take a closer look at a matter of exegesis that establishes our argument; and third, a brief examination will be made of the implications that ensue for the Christian life.

THE QUESTION OF MIND

Harry Blamires addressed some aspects of our question in his interesting and important book, *The Christian Mind: How Should a Christian Think?* some forty years ago.[4] But Blamires begins with the conclusion that "There is no longer a Christian mind."[5] His quite valuable argument is substantially preoccupied with the respects in which he claims that "as a *thinking* being, the modern Christian has succumbed to secularization." That follows his suggestion that "There is no longer a Christian mind. [but] There is still, of course, a Christian ethic."[6] That the thought of the Christian about the affairs of life must necessarily be different from that of the world is, of course, important in itself. But Blamires' suggestion that a "Christian ethic" remains viable when "there is no longer a Christian mind" threatens to be vacuous. For it is possible thereby to fall into a trap that has been glaringly apparent since twentieth-century thought turned its back on Christian doctrinal imperatives. It is the trap of imagining that in the world at large the Christian ethic is supportable without the Christian doctrine.

Mark Noll has also addressed aspects of our question, but in his *The Scandal of the Evangelical Mind* he begins with the conclusion that "The scandal of the evangelical mind is that there is not much of an evangelical mind."[7] What Noll means by "the life of the mind" is not concerned primarily with "theology as such,"[8] he says, but with "the effort to think like

---

4. Blamires, *The Christian Mind*. See also the same author's *Recovering the Christian Mind*, and *The PostChristian Mind*.
5. Blamires, *The Christian Mind*, 3.
6. Idem.
7. Noll, *Scandal of the Evangelical Mind*, 3.
8. Ibid., 6.

a Christian—to think within a specifically Christian framework—across the whole spectrum of modern learning."[9] That statement recalls the fairly widespread clamor in recent times for the development of what is referred to as a Christian worldview. But in the strained complex and wavering state of contemporary theology and the shallowness of the church, the claims of a Christian worldview are frequently more concerned with the meaning of the noun than with a clear understanding of the adjective.[10] While, of course, to think Christianly lies at the basis of correct Christian living, again it has to be said that our more fundamental concern directs us to the question of precisely what is to be said of the Christian mind in and of itself. The answer to that question, we shall go on to see, lies precisely in the apostle's claim that "we have the mind of Christ."

Our perspective is determined by the reality of the injury imposed on the mind by Adam's fall. For Adam in his created state, to be was to know. He naturally knew God and knew that he had come from the hands of God. But his fall consisted essentially in his asserting a false autonomy of mind and in the assumption that he could sovereignly find the categories of meaning within himself or within the context of culture in which he came to self-awareness. Adam responded to the suggestions of the tempter with the assertion that he would believe neither the claims of God nor the claims of the devil. He would, he asserted, decide for himself. He would himself be the arbiter of his destiny. That very initial Adamic assertion involved the claim of the autonomy of the human mind. Adam effectively denied his creaturehood, in that whatever might be said as to his origin, he asserted that he could henceforth proceed, in thought and in life, as though he was not dependent on what God has declared to be valid criteria of truth and the meaning of the created laws of being and function. But it is important to recognize that in the fall the faculty of mind was not destroyed or obliterated. Adam's fall was primarily an ethical lapse, not a metaphysical lapse, in that his faculty of thought as well as his faculty of emotion and will remained. The fall was an ethical lapse in that Adam did what he should not have done. He ate the forbidden fruit. But involved in the human status that resulted was the fact that a terrible bias was introduced into the soul. Man could still, and he does still, think. He remains the image of God. But his thought now runs on a crooked

---

9. Ibid., 7.
10. Valuable background reading is contained in Naugle, *Worldview*.

track. A bias of soul prevents his seeing or knowing or understanding anything of the redemptive revelation of God. He may suppose *that* God is, in doing so conjecturing a god made in his own image. But he does not know and cannot know *who* God is. Indeed, his bias of soul prevents his true understanding of anything within the range of created reality. His thought is necessarily and inevitably apostate, unless and until the new life of God in Christ is created within him by the regenerating grace of the Spirit of God. Man, in his existential claims, in his thought and in his actions in the world, is a covenant-breaker (Rom 1:30–31).

We speak of the "priority of the intellect." We mean by that in our present context that as the faculty of mind in man's initially created state was the prince of the faculties of the soul, so now, as man remains the image of God and by reason that his faculty of mind is accessible to God, the first appeal of the gospel is to the mind. God calls upon men everywhere to repent (Acts 17:30), and the meaning of repentance is essentially a change of mind. It is a call to think again, now with a new capacity of understanding born in the soul by the Holy Spirit's grace of regeneration. The meaning of what has just been said is clarified by the awareness that now, in the fallen state in which he naturally exists apart from the grace of God, man's sorry condition is characterized by the fact that the primeval hegemony of the mind has been replaced by the hegemony of the emotions. Man in sin now does what he wants to do. He does what he likes. He is now a law unto himself. There is no fear of God before his eyes. We shall refer again to the meaning of sin and sinful action. It will be necessary to see the meaning of sin even in the lives of those who "have the mind of Christ." We shall see therein the paradox of the Christian faith and life. But in the shortest of terms and with pointed summary, sin is essentially and at its root the repudiation of covenantal obligations. Again, man in sin is a covenant breaker. And sin, for the sinner, is always self-referential. It is a love of self. For the sinner, a love of self has displaced the love of God.

But if, now, the regenerate man has "the mind of Christ," it remains to ask whether, to advert to our previous categories, a change has occurred in man's ontological status. Our short answer is in the negative. For in the same way as we said a moment ago that the fall was an ethical, and not a metaphysical, lapse, so now we say that there is no metaphysical change involved in the Spirit's movement of an individual to a regenerate state. The man remains the same metaphysical being he was before. What is involved in regeneration is not the creation of new faculties of soul, but the endowment of the existing faculties with abilities and capacities they did not previously possess. And with those newly endowed faculties the man is now freed to know, to love, and to obey God. If, to expand the thought, we say that the fall was essentially ethical, not metaphysical, are we to say that regeneration is again primarily ethical? There is good reason to pursue the thought. But what is involved in regeneration and in the new endowments of capacities of soul it implies is that the individual who is the beneficiary of that grace is now enabled to live and perform on a totally new ethical level. The regenerate man is the same man. But he now enjoys new ethical capacities and proclivities. As to the regenerate man's existential status, while, as has been said, there has been no metaphysical change, no change in his status of responsible being and personhood, the regenerating operation of the Spirit of God within the soul establishes the person in a new, vital, spiritual, and indissoluble union with Christ.

The statement we have just made as to regenerate being and consciousness illumines further the meaning of one's participation in "the mind of Christ." For we now see that it remains quite outside the realm of possibility that the human person could share in any ontological identity with Christ. Regeneration does not mean or involve one's absorption into the divine essence. Regeneration, again, is not ontological. It does not imply or accomplish the divinization of man. It is true that the apostle Peter has said that by the will and power of God those to whom the grace of regeneration has been given are made "partakers of the divine nature" (2 Pet 1:4). But what is involved in Peter's claim is that by the will and grace of God there is communicated to the Christian some degree of the communicable attributes of God. That communication is, in fact, a divinely ordered aspect of the Christian believer's progress in sanctification. We can say that the communicable attributes of God, aspects of the "divine nature," are communicated to the believer in the degree that, and to the extent that, he is being prepared for the place God has ordained he will occupy in the eternal kingdom of glory.

To put the issue in simplest terms, to have the mind of Christ means that one learns to think on all levels, about all levels of value, about things spiritual and mundane, things common and things holy, as Christ thinks. One has the mind of Christ in that he begins to see the meaning of what God has declared in the same way as Christ sees it. Sin now begins to mean to him what it means to Christ, and the entire compass of God's redemption begins to appear to him as Christ sees the meaning of the redemption he accomplished. We say that the regenerate person *begins* to see all these things as Christ sees them, because we know that on all levels of knowledge and understanding man's achievement is an analogical replica of the unfathomable divine knowledge. Man can know these things truly, but not comprehensively.

Again, to have the mind of Christ is to know what Christ has said and what he directs us to as the requirements of holy living. The ambassador for a king knows with careful thoroughness what he has been commissioned to convey as the wishes or edicts of the king. As he knows what the king has said and intended and commissioned, he can be said to know, or have, the mind of the king. So it is with the Christian believer. He has the mind of Christ in that he has been privileged to know to progressive degrees the mind of Christ, what Christ has thought and said and mandated.

But lying behind what has been said is the very nature of the mind of Christ, the mind that is in Christ, the knowledge and the knowing of Christ, as that is to be conceived of in his divine and human natures. In briefest terms we can say with the Chalcedonian settlement that in Christ the divine and the human natures are joined in union without confusion, without change, without division, and without separation.[11] It is necessary to see in the light of that the remarkable salvific import of the human nature of Christ. In short, it was in his human nature that our Lord rendered obedience to the law and suffered and died for us, and in his human nature he discharges his heavenly high priestly office on our behalf. We shall in due time see him in the same, but glorified, human nature in the great day of his appearing, and we shall see God in him in human nature through all eternity. The angels said to the disciples on the occasion of our Lord's ascension, "[T]his same Jesus, which is taken up from you into heaven, shall so come *in like manner* as ye have seen him go into heaven" (Acts 1:11, italics added).

When we say, then, that the divine and the human natures of Christ were joined in the manner that Chalcedon articulated, we are saying that

---

11. The so-called "Chalcedonian settlement," as that is explained in the following paragraphs of the text above, was the outcome of the Council of Chalcedon in 451AD. The final settlement at that time as to the Person and the divine and human natures of Christ was a culmination of doctrinal discussions in three preceding councils: Nicea in 325, Constantinople in 381, and Ephesus in 435.

following our Lord's incarnation there exists within his Personhood both a divine mind and a human mind, both a divine will and a human will, and all the faculties of human soul that we possess by nature. But the union involved did not mean that Christ was, or became, a human person. He was, and he remained, a divine Person, not a human person, and not a divine-human person. In him, as Berkhof has put it, the human nature "was not personalized."[12] The reality of his Personhood challenges our adoration. The reality of our Lord's human nature informs his understanding of us as he sees and succors us in the journey we take until we arrive with him in glory. That is because in his human nature he "was in all points tempted like as we are" (Heb 4:15).

If there had been any confusion of the divine and human natures of Christ, or if, that is, it were supposed that in his person he was monophysite,[13] it could have been said also, as an old heresy attempted to claim, that Christ was monothelite.[14] That would say that he was a person who had only one will. But that, we have seen, is not so. As to our Lord's divine nature, moreover, it is not the case that the blessed triune Persons of the Godhead share in the divine essence in the sense that that essence is distributed among or between them. For the full essence of the Godhead resides fully in each of the Persons. The divine mind, it has therefore to be said, is wholly in the Father, wholly in the Son, and wholly in the Holy Spirit. Again, the divine will is fully in each of the Persons. Our mediator is himself God. Our Lord himself made the definitive statement to that effect when he said, "I and my Father are one" (John 10:30). The "one" in that statement is in the neuter gender, indicating that oneness of substance is in view. We hold to trinitarian consubstantiality. The Westminster Shorter Catechism has made the point in its statement that "There are three persons in the Godhead; the Father, the Son, and the Holy Ghost; and these three are one God, *the same in substance*, equal in power and glory."[15]

---

12. Berkhof, *Systematic Theology*, 322.

13. See Shedd, *History*, vol. 1, 397 for a discussion of monophysitism, or the supposed loss of the duality of the divine and human natures in Christ.

14. For discussions of monothelitism (which was condemned by the Council of Constantinople in 680AD) see Shedd, *Dogmatic Theology*, vol. 2, 328, and Hodge, *Systematic Theology*, vol. 2, 405.

15. Westminster Shorter Catechism, Question 6, italics added.

A MATTER OF EXEGESIS

The statement of Paul to the Corinthians that has engaged us reflects that of the prophet Isaiah who asks: "Who hath directed the Spirit of the Lord, or being his counseller hath taught him" (Isa 40:13). We observe three terms in Isaiah's question: First, the Spirit [or the mind] of God; second, the possibility of a counseller to God; and third, the possibility of one's being a teacher of God. It is of interest that at Romans 11:34 Paul adopts the first and the second of those clauses, "For who hath known the mind of the Lord?" and "[W]ho hath been his counseller?" Now at 1 Corinthians 2:16 Paul adopts the first and the third of Isaiah's clauses, "For who hath known the mind of the Lord, that he may instruct him?" On the very surface of the text two things are at issue. First, we have clearly before us the prophetic and the apostolic statements that God (implying the being and the knowledge of God, meaning thereby the knowledge that God possesses), is incomprehensible to us. And second, we have the equally clear identification of God who had revealed himself to the prophets and Christ who came as the Lord of the covenant to redeem the people of God. Again, Christ is fully God. When it is said, then, that we have the mind of Christ, we see as before that we know and realize something of the depth of the meaning of the things that God himself has revealed. We know those things because God has conveyed to us the anological replica of his own knowledge, to the degree and to the extent that we are able by his grace to comprehend. We know them because we begin to know what the Second Person of the Godhead came into the world to reveal to us. We are said to have his mind because, as has been said, we now begin to know how and what he thinks, what is the substance of his redemptive purpose and the larger terms of his covenantal objectives.

It will assist the further understanding of the apostle's claim that "we have the mind of Christ" to consider again in its larger context the successive clauses in the 1 Corinthians 2:16 text. In particular, our focus at this point is on the clause, "that he may instruct him." Paul had put the question, "who hath known the mind of the Lord," and then follows "that he may instruct him." Now in Isaiah's question that has informed the apostle's statement the "him" in the clause "who hath taught him" clearly has reference to "the Spirit of the Lord." The "him" is, then, God. Our question now is who is the "him" that is in view in the apostle's statement to the Corinthians when he asks "who may instruct him?" While Isaiah's text clearly underlies that in the Corinthian letter, the question is to be asked whether the "him" in the latter refers to God, or here the Lord, or, rather, or perhaps additionally by implication, to the Christian man who is now the beneficiary of the enlightenment that Christ has imparted to him.

The answer to that question may be influenced by the preceding context of the Pauline letter. In the preceding verses Paul differentiated between those who were still in the darkness of ignorance and sin and the man who was now able to discern and to know the spiritual things of God. Indeed, the former were so blind, Paul says, that they ignorantly crucified the Lord of glory (1 Cor 2:8). They crucified Christ in ignorance of what they were doing. "[F]or had they known it, they would not have crucified the Lord of glory." They didn't know what they were doing. They were sincere in their action, but they were sincerely wrong. But their action and their ignorance were culpable. Paul's argument then moves beyond those people to speak of the critical difference of those who have received "not the spirit of the world, but the spirit which is of God." They, Paul says, know "the things that are freely given to us of God" (1 Cor 2:12). That advance in knowledge occurs because such people now have not "the words which man's wisdom teacheth, but which the Holy Ghost teacheth; comparing spiritual things with spiritual." The two classes of people are in view throughout Paul's discussion.

The apostle's thought is thereby propelled to his conclusion that when the two different individuals are compared, "the natural man receiveth not the things of the Spirit of God; for they are foolishness unto him; neither can he know them, because they are spiritually discerned" (1 Cor 2:14). But now a special and unique status is accorded the spiritual person. Contrary to the blindness and ignorance and incapacity of the natural man, contrary to his inability to make meaningful judgments of spiritual realities, it is to be said of the spiritual man that "he that is spiritual . . . is judged of no man" (1 Cor 2:15). The exegetical question now before us turns on the respect in which that conclusion of verse 15 carries an import into the verse that follows. As it stands at that point, Paul has reached almost the end of his argument. He has reached the point of making it clear that no person who has not been enlightened by the Spirit of God is able to stand in judgment on the spiritual man, the man who is the beneficiary of the teaching of the Spirit of God. The argument throughout has been focused on the characteristics, the capacities, and the prerogatives of the two different classes of men, the one natural and the other spiritual.

We focus our thought at this stage on what the apostle insists on at that point. No unenlightened person is competent to understand, or stand in judgment on, the regenerate individual. That is because the latter has the mind of Christ and the former does not. When, then, the argument follows that the man of the world cannot "instruct" the man of God, the question returns as to who is the "him" referred to in 1 Corinthians 2:16? Our answer is, of course, that on a level that directly reflects Isaiah's text the "him" must be God himself. But a study of the apostle's context, which contains a consistent differentiation between the natural and the spiritual person, suggests that a reference to the regenerate man is also intended. That conclusion will inform, then, what is to be said regarding the implications of the text for the status, the texture, the conduct, and the benefits of the Christian life. We shall return to that significant implication.

Of course no mere man can instruct God. No man can instruct Christ. But we are interested also in the remarkable implication that no mere natural man can understand and instruct the one who has now been raised to the status of union with Christ. That is because the latter now has "the mind of Christ." What a remarkable status it is to which the man in Christ has been raised. Why is that so? The apostle was never tired of giving the answer. It was because, as he put it to the Galatian church, "I live; yet not I, but Christ liveth in me" (Gal 2:20). The great doctrine and fact of our union with Christ demands our closest attention and should motivate our eternal thanks to God for what Paul referred to in another place as his "unspeakable gift" (2 Cor 9:15).[16]

It is of interest that the old Puritan commentator, Matthew Henry, has observed insightfully on the question now before us. The one who is "spiritually minded" (1 Cor 2:15), Henry observes, "has a relish and savour of divine truths; he sees divine wisdom, and experiences divine power, in gospel revelations and mysteries, which the carnal and unsanctified mind looks upon as weakness and folly, as things destitute of all power and not worthy of any regard." That is the difference between the two classes of men. Henry continues: "He that is spiritual (who has had divine revelations made to him, receives them as such, and founds his faith and religion upon them) . . . can discern what is, and what is not, the doctrine

---

16. See the discussion of the Christian believer's union with Christ in Vickers, *When God Converts a Sinner*, chapter 7.

of the gospel and of salvation." But the operative question that follows, taking up the issues explored in 1 Corinthians 2:16, is, as Henry states it, *"For who hath known the mind of the Lord, that he may instruct him* (v.16), that is, the *spiritual man?"* Note Henry's reference there to the "him" in verse 16 as the spiritual man. Henry continues, "Who can enter so far into the mind of God, as to instruct him who has the Spirit of God and is under his inspiration? He only is the person to whom God immediately communicates the knowledge of his will."[17] Henry, as we have noted, has suggested the significant sense in which the "him" in 1 Corinthians 2:16 can be understood by implication to apply to the regenerate Christian man. It applies to him because he has the mind of Christ.

Charles Hodge reaches a similar conclusion. The statement in I Corinthians 2:16, he concludes, follows as "a confirmation of what precedes." He then summarizes by saying that "Syllogistically stated, the argument would stand thus: No one can instruct the Lord. We have the mind of the Lord. Therefore no one can instruct or judge us."[18]

Let me summarize 1 Corinthians 2:16, then, as follows. The question is: Who has known the mind of the Lord (verse 16) in such a way as to be able to understand or instruct the "spiritual man" (verse 15)? Answer: We who are spiritual, but only we who are spiritual, because we *do* know the mind of the Lord, because "we have the mind of Christ."[19]

The deduction before us is that the union between Christ and the Christian is of such a close and existential nature that no natural man can now be the instructor of either Christ or the Christian. The natural man cannot begin to understand the status or the ethic of the man in Christ.

---

17. See Henry, *Commentary,* loc. cit.

18. Hodge, *Commentary,* 45.

19. With reference to this entire line of analysis, and to the "him" in 1 Corinthians 2:16, see Fee, *The First Epistle to the Corinthians,* 119. Fee comments, "in the context of the argument this probably has a double intent.... it simply asks rhetorically of the *psychikoi* how they can expect to know true wisdom, *and thereby pass judgment on the one who has the Spirit,* when they do not have the mind of the Lord" (italics added). At the same time, Fee continues, it "is directed now at his [Paul's] Corinthian friends themselves." Thiselton, in his *The First Epistle to the Corinthians,* 274, refers positively to Fee's "double intent" and observes that "the quotation in v. 16 ... can also be attributed equally to the Corinthian 'spiritual persons.'" That is, it is the Christian who has "known the mind of the Lord," because, as the text says, he has "the mind of Christ." It is, then, only he who can, as Fee puts it, "pass judgment on the one who has the Spirit."

The two live and move in completely disparate realms so far as true meaning and eternal verities are concerned.

THE QUESTION OF ETHICS

The question before us now has to do with the implications for the life and conduct of the Christian of the fact that he has the mind of Christ. After a preliminary point of summary of our argument we shall submit a number of propositions that bear on that question.

We stated at an earlier point that we were challenged to see the relations between Christian ontology, epistemology, and ethics. Ontology, or the question of being, we concluded, was prior to epistemology or the question of knowledge. That was because, as we put it, the "what" of knowledge is prior to the "how" of knowledge. The theological significance of that conclusion rests in the fact that only because God is, and because he has spoken and thereby provided the foundation of the "what" of knowledge or of what there is to be known, is it possible to know anything at all. Our further conclusion at this stage is that ontology and epistemology are prior to ethics. By that we mean, in short, two things. First, what a man is, as to his being or his ontic condition as that is further characterized by either regenerate or unregenerate status, determines what he does. Or again, we say that being is prior to doing. Second, the nature and quality of that behavior is determined by what a man knows. We do not mean by that, in the sense of classic Greek thought, that to know the good is to do the good. We mean, rather, that in varying respects what a person knows guides his action and that, in the case of the Christian person in particular, his possession of the mind of Christ most definitely is, or as we shall see, should be, a guide to behavior. In what ways, then, is the Christian's possession of the mind of Christ determinative of action, conduct, and life? Several relevant propositions follow.

> **First proposition:** *If a person possesses the mind of Christ, that possession is the result of the selective ordination of God.*

It is not necessary to open at length at this point the large and foundational doctrines of the predestination, election, sovereignty, and providence of God. But three points can be made. First, we hold to the aseity of God, that he is without cause external to himself, and that as to his being and his knowledge he is not dependent on any entity or law or possibility outside of himself. God knows himself and knows all things external to himself that he spoke into existence in one eternal act of knowing. To say otherwise is to speak of a god unknown to the Scriptures. By reason that God has established all of the being and laws of operation of reality external to himself, we hold that all of that being and all of those laws are the property of God. Because that property rests in God he is able to, and he does, do with that property whatsoever he wills. That means that as to all eventuation within created reality God knows the end from the beginning. He does not wait to discover. We reject the claims of the contemporary theology of "open theism" that holds, in essence, that God does not know, but waits to discover and to react to, the future in real time and history. We say, to the contrary, that his knowledge is not sequentially acquired. He knows sequences, but as Dabney has put it, he does not know sequences sequentially.[20] God is therefore sovereign, and he will not bequeath, convey, or delegate that sovereignty to any man. By reason of God's sovereignty and authority he is free to communicate or not communicate to his fallen creatures made in his image a redemptive knowledge of himself. Those who are the recipients of that knowledge have the mind of Christ. That is, they are those whom God freely chooses to call and endow with the mind of Christ.

Second, it follows that personal salvation, or, again, the communication of the mind of Christ, is the result or effect of a divine monergism. The Arminian theology argues to the contrary. It holds essentially to a *human* monergism, or to varying forms of divine-human synergism. It was the signal achievement of the Reformation theology that it transmuted the semi-Pelagianism of Rome back to a biblical theology of the sovereign grace and disposal of God. Salvation, it rediscovered, was entirely due, in all its parts and in all its aspects and processes, to the grace of God.

Third, by reason of the fallen state in which all men exist as a result of Adam's fall, no individual person has, or could have had, any claim on God's redemptive mercy. We say that those possess the mind of Christ whom God sovereignly endows with the mind of Christ because of the true remarkableness of God's ordination to that effect. The remarkable thing is not that God, in his survey of fallen men and their universal entitlement to perdition, failed to choose everybody to salvation. The remarkable thing is that he sovereignly chose any.

---

20. Dabney, *Discussions*, vol. 1, 294. Compare Edwards, *Freedom of the Will*, Morgan, PA edition, 144, "[T]here is no succession in God's knowledge."

Second proposition: *Because God's communication of the mind of Christ is his sovereign disposal, no individual can be proud of his election.*

The proposition is sustained by what has already been said. If any man were able to find any merit in himself that warranted the saving grace of God he could take some satisfaction in that reality. But any such pride of self is precluded by the state of sin and potential perdition in which all stand apart from the grace of God. We reject, that is, the false Roman doctrine of congruent grace, an element of Rome's semi-Pelagianism, that precedes the gift of salvation. Those to whom the mind of Christ has been communicated know that the only action worthy of their standing in Christ is a humility that bows before the God of grace in confession of their complete lack of merit and thankfulness for the grace of God administered to them.

Third proposition: *The possession of the mind of Christ does not imply perfection or completeness of knowledge or the cognition of all that is to be known.*

It is of the essence of the God-man relation that God has made a self-disclosure to man. God has revealed himself in many ways—in creation; in man himself, who is properly understood only as he is seen to be revelatory of God; in history, particularly, but not only, in redemptive history; in the Scriptures; and finally in his Son (Heb 1:1–2). "No man hath seen God at any time; the only begotten Son . . . hath declared him" (John 1:18). The Son of God came into this world to become Jesus Christ in order to be the declarer of the Father. Christ said to Philip who had asked, "Lord, show us the Father," that "he that hath seen me hath seen the Father" (John 14:8–9).

But God's revelation to man is a partial revelation. That follows necessarily from what we have observed as the incomprehensibility of God and of the knowledge of God, the knowledge that God possesses of himself and of his purposes of eventuation in the world. For when we say that the knowledge available to us is analogical of God's knowledge we hold that there is a qualitative, and not merely a quantitative, difference between God's knowledge and our knowledge. Further, the revelation that God has recorded in the Scriptures is a partial record of the partial revelation that he has, in fact, made. If all his revelation had been recorded there would not have been enough books in the world to contain it (John 21:25). But further still, our understanding of the partial inscripturation of God's partial revelation is, at best, a partial comprehension. It is partial, but, happily, progressive for those who sincerely commit to Christ.

When we say, then, that we have the mind of Christ, we realize that we at this stage know only in part. At best we see through a glass darkly (1 Cor 13:12). The Christian man is engaged on a process of sequential learning and expanding comprehension.

> **Fourth proposition**: *The possession of the mind of Christ means that the understanding of Christian truth, of God's redemptive purpose and the outworking of its effects in life, has in the present state only begun.*

That follows from what has just been said. We observed at an earlier point that to possess the mind of Christ means that we thereby *begin* to understand the Christian's true status and the benefits that flow from it. Now it can be said further that the Holy Spirit of God progressively ministers to his saints the fuller sense of what it means to know him and to increase in the awareness of his presence in their lives. In other words, it is the assignment and task of the Holy Spirit, the redemptive office that he undertook in the predeterminate council of the Godhead, to communicate to those whom Christ redeemed the gifts and benefits that he purchased for them. By the sovereign ministry of the Spirit the people of God progress in sanctification. But in this life sanctification has only begun. The saints will be completely conformed to the holiness that is in Christ only at the day of his appearing. But when we bring into focus in this way the partial and progressive nature of our sanctification we at the same time hold to two aspects of it. First, God is again sovereign in sanctification, as he reserves to himself sovereignty in all aspects of salvation. And second, the degree to which God thus communicates his blessing of sanctification is precisely consistent with his objectives of our sainthood and his will for us.

> **Fifth proposition:** *The possession of the mind of Christ does not carry with it freedom from sin.*

It is an all too present reality that perfect conformity to the holiness to which God calls us is unavailable to us in this short, uncertain life and earthly pilgrimage. The apostle has made that clear in his own case in the seventh chapter of his letter to the Romans. "O wretched man that I am," he exclaims. And we know with too much familiarity the presence of sin in our own lives. Is it not true that the increasing consciousness of sanctification is accompanied by an increasing consciousness of sin and sensitivity to sin? Is it not true to say that it is the most advanced saint who is most consciously aware of the meaning of sin? Why else did the writer to the Hebrews say, when he reminded us of the cloud of witnesses in whose view we live, "[L]et us lay aside every weight, and the sin which doth so easily beset us, and let us run with patience the race that is set before us" (Heb 12:1)?

The explanation of sin in the life of the believer turns on his imperfect grasp of the meaning of the remarkable fact that we have explored at length, namely that he has the mind of Christ. A lethargy and indolence too often drags us down from the heights of grace to which God calls us and which he waits to share with us. Did he not say "I stand at the door and knock: If any man hear my voice, and open the door, I will come in to him, and sup with him" (Rev 3:20)? At issue in our Lord's declaration is the fact that he wants to share with us the blessings of sanctification to which he calls us. He wants to be more consistently present in our lives. But too often we ignore him. We learn only slightly the yearning love of the spouse in Solomon's Song who was conscious of desolation when she had lost the presence of her Lord.

Sin in the life of the believer is explained, not only by the temptations and subtleties of the devil without, the enemy and adversary of the soul who can readily present himself as an angel of light, but by the residue of sinful propensities within. John Owen addressed the issue in his *Discourse Concerning the Holy Spirit* and spoke of the "remaining contrary dispositions and inclinations" within those "who are constantly inclined and disposed unto all the acts of a heavenly, spiritual life."[21] Those inclinations to sin proceed, Owen concludes, "from the *remainders* of a contrary habitual principle. This the Scripture calls ... the 'sin that dwelleth in us.'"[22]

But there is a remedy for sin. "If we confess our sins, he is faithful and just to forgive us our sins, and to cleanse us from all unrighteousness" (1 John 1:9). "[I]f any man sin, we have an advocate with the Father, Jesus Christ the righteous" (1 John 2:1). The fact and realization of "the mind of Christ" carries with it a clear imperative. "[I]f we walk in the light, as he is in the light, we have fellowship one with another" (1 John 1:7). The apostle

---

21. Owen, *Discourse Concerning the Holy Spirit*, in *Works*, vol. 3, 488.

22. Idem. See also for comment on Owen's "contrary habitual principle," Ferguson, *John Owen on the Christian Life*, 64.

clearly intends thereby, as he had said in his same paragraph, "fellowship with the Father" (1 John 1:3).

> **Sixth proposition:** *It is not possible for any man, and certainly not possible for the Christian, to think any thought that God has not already thought.*

It is not possible or necessary to explore at length at this stage all that the proposition implies. The principal objection to it is that it controverts the assumption of human free will. Let it be said that any attempt to maintain the argument for free will runs into a dead end at the point at which account must be taken of the overriding sovereignty of the providence of God. At this point it is sufficient to say that there comes into view a further implication of the fact that, as the apostle has said, we have the mind of Christ. We have spoken at length of what that means as the Christian comprehends the fact of the endowment that he thereby possesses. And we have spoken of the Spirit's progressive administration to the Christian of the grace of sanctification. Our present proposition can be seen as a statement of a significant aspect of that administration of the Spirit. God moves in the very thought life of the Christian, as he moves in the surrounding elements of his life experience, to move him forward in the very sanctification he mandates. God the Holy Spirit, that is, gives to the Christian what God demands. It would be inadequate to say that the Spirit orders only the external events and experiences in the life of the individual he is committed to bring to glory. The Spirit moves in the innermost recesses of the soul. He thinks the thoughts of holiness in us, and he thereby structures our lives and our progress. What else would be the meaning and import of the apostle's exclamation to the Galatians, "I live; yet not I, but Christ liveth in me" (Gal 2:20)? The hymn writer, Harriet Auber, as we noted previously, has captured the meaning of what is involved in the hymn that begins, "Our blest Redeemer, ere He breathed/ His tender, last farewell,/ A guide, a comforter, bequeathed/ With us to dwell." And in the penultimate stanza of the hymn the writer reflects on the ministry to the soul of that Comforter and states significantly that "Every thought of holiness [is] his alone."[23]

---

23. Auber, *Our blest Redeemer, ere He breathed His tender, last farewell*, in Congregational Praise, 209.

Seventh proposition: *The Christian's possession of the mind of Christ carries with it heavy obligations for conduct and behavior.*

A number of relevant points implicit in the proposition can be summarized. First, the proposition brings to emphasis the meaning of Christian covenantal obligation that should determine the Christian's ethic. We said at an earlier stage that the meaning of sin in its essential import is that sin is the repudiation of covenantal obligations. The primeval sin that "brought death into the world and all our woe"[24] was a clear repudiation of the obligations to which Adam was committed under the covenant of works. Indeed, all men ever since have remained subject to the obligations of that covenant. The meaning of the redemption that Christ provided is that he did for us what were obligated to do under it but were unable to do for ourselves. Christ fulfilled for us our unfulfilled obligations under the covenant of works. It is in that sense that he is our covenantal substitute. We are conscious that not only is man a covenantal creature, not only is creation covenantally structured, but that we stand under the sovereign God with obligations that the covenants of God impose on us. It is sufficient to say that we now, as the beneficiaries of the covenant of grace, are similarly conscious of the obligations that the benefits of that covenant place upon us.

Second, the consciousness of our covenantal status as the redeemed people of God makes us acutely aware of God's purpose in his covenantal communication to us of the mind of Christ. That purpose is encapsulated in the apostle's declaration that God "hath chosen us in him [Christ] before the foundation of the world, that we should be holy and without blame before him in love; Having predestinated us unto the adoption of children by Jesus Christ to himself . . . To the praise of the glory of his grace" (Eph 1:4–5). And Peter again underlines the purpose, and therefore the obligations upon us that are correlative with it: "But ye are a chosen generation . . . an holy nation . . . that ye should show forth the praises of him who hath called you out of darkness into his marvellous light" (1 Pet 2:9).

Third, it is part of the Christian's responsibility to recognize the means of grace that God has provided, which in themselves are conducive to the ends that sanctification envisages—submission to the Word of God;

---

24. Milton, *Paradise Lost*, line 3.

continuance in prayer; attendance to the preaching of the Word; attendance to, and appreciation for, the fellowship of the saints; and the proper administration of the sacraments. It is part of the obligations placed upon us as possessors of the mind of Christ to protect the proper worship of his church. We acknowledge that the church is in the world to announce the gospel of salvation. But we have been slow to recognize that the world has crept into the church. We have been too ready to capitulate to the idioms of the world and the behavior norms of the world in the structure and conduct of what we imagine is proper worship. We have forgotten that God has laid down clearly in his word how he wishes to be worshipped. The issues multiply.

Finally, the obligations we sustain as God's people who have been endowed with "the mind of Christ" are summed up in the injunction that because we are his people we must be like him. The mandate is spread liberally across the pages of Scripture. Let us ask of ourselves, is it our wish to strive to be like our Lord who has saved us? Are we diligent in following him? Do we feel any dismay when for our lethargy he withdraws from us the consciousness of his presence? Does the thought of him fashion our everyday and motivate all that we would know and desire and do.

Let us ask our final question in a different way. God has set his love upon us. Not that we loved him, but that he loved us (1 John 4:10) and, as the hymn writer, James Small, says, "He drew me with the cords of love, and thus he bound me to him."[25] But do we return, with honest affection, that eternal and gracious love? God grant that it may be so.

---

25. Small, *I've found a friend, O such a friend*, in Trinity Hymnal, 517.

7

The Justification of Christ?

THE QUESTION MARK I have included in the title of this chapter reacts to some recent attempts to effect paradigm changes in Reformed theology.[1] In the context of our discussion of saving faith the question pressing for attention is that of who, or what, is the *object* of saving faith. If, as Reformed thought has consistently claimed, the object of saving faith is the Lord Jesus Christ, the question remains as to why and how that is so. What in other words, is to be said of the Person of Christ to whom saving faith is presumably directed, and what is it in his presence and work in this world, his perfect obedience, his sacrificial dereliction, his resurrection, ascension, and heavenly session that provides a sure warrant for saving faith? Or again, to put the question in the language of certain contemporary claims, is saving faith effective for justification because Christ himself was "justified" by and at his resurrection? What, as my title suggests, are we to say of the justification of Christ?

The fourteenth chapter of the Westminster Confession of Faith (1647) notes clearly the conjunction of saving faith and justification. "The principal acts of saving faith," it states, "are, accepting, receiving, and resting upon Christ alone for justification, sanctification, and eternal life, by virtue of the covenant of grace."[2] In that statement Pauline theology is faithfully reproduced. But in the context of the doctrinal issues we are now discussing, the proper construction of Pauline theology has itself

---

1. I have discussed some of those attempts at paradigm change in chapter 7 of *When God Converts a Sinner*.

2. Westminster Confession of Faith, XIV:2. The Savoy Declaration of Faith (1658) contains the same statement in its chapter 14. The Second London (Baptist) Confession (1689), also in its chapter 14, contains a similar statement but eliminates the word "are" in the definition and substitutes the weaker "have immediate relation to Christ," though it continues with "accepting, receiving, and resting upon him alone ..." as in Westminster and Savoy.

been called in question. Consider, for example, the claim of a prominent and influential contemporary Reformed theologian, Richard Gaffin: "Not justification by faith but union with the resurrected Christ by faith (of which union, to be sure, the justifying aspect stands out perhaps most prominently) is the central motif of Paul's applied soteriology."[3] Gaffin shifts the "central motif of Paul's soteriology" from what might have been thought to be the cross of Christ and the divine transaction that was effected there to the resurrection that followed. He underlines his perspective by claiming that "The central soteriological reality is union with the exalted Christ by Spirit-created faith. That is the nub, the essence, of the way or order of salvation for Paul."[4] Left aside for the moment are Paul's assertions that "I determined not to know anything among you, save Jesus Christ, and him crucified" (1 Cor 2:2), and "God forbid that I should glory, save in the cross of our Lord Jesus Christ" (Gal 6:14).[5]

Gaffin's doctrinal reconstructions, as we shall observe, have come under question by other Reformed theologians. But it can be noted at this point that he maintains his concentration on the believer's union with Christ because, as he argues, "That union also has judicial or forensic significance, *as does Christ's own resurrection.*"[6] By that he means that "Christ's resurrection is his own justification,"[7] and "the resurrection is . . . Christ's justification or the point of entering into a state of being justified."[8] The sense in which union with Christ thus becomes the central coordinating motif in Gaffin's theology follows from his reference to "The resurrection as the redemption of Christ,"[9] and similarly, "the resurrection of Jesus

---

3. Gaffin, *Resurrection and Redemption*, 132.

4. Gaffin, *By Faith, not by Sight*, 43. It is noteworthy, as a fuller examination of Gaffin's doctrinal orientation reveals, that he has substantially rejected the classic Reformed *ordo salutis* construction of the application of salvation.

5. See a further discussion of Gaffin's doctrinal claims in my *When God Converts a Sinner*, chapter 7.

6. Gaffin, *By Faith, not by Sight*, 84, italics added.

7. Idem.

8. Gaffin, *Resurrection and Redemption*, 121.

9. Ibid., 114.

is his *adoption*,"[10] "Jesus' resurrection is his justification,"[11] and "Christ's resurrection [is] his sanctification."[12]

In the debates that have followed from such claims, much turns on what is at issue in the conception of the "redemption of Christ." We shall return to the point, particularly as it relates to the perceived justificatory aspect of Christ's resurrection. Gaffin is undoubtedly correct to wrestle with the relation between the death and the resurrection of Christ on the one hand and the justification of the sinner on the other. But in the light of his overall soteriology a question arises regarding the scope of the accomplishment of redemption in its most comprehensive sense. What meaning and implication are to be attached, in that larger context, to the perceived redemption of Christ?

Gaffin responds that it is "not only meaningful but necessary to speak of the resurrection as the redemption of Christ" because "The resurrection is . . . his deliverance from the power and curse of death which was in force until the moment of being raised."[13] It is a clear statement of faith that "Christ's humiliation consisted in his . . . being buried and continuing under the power of death for a time."[14] It is again clearly stated and believed that Christ bore the wrath of God due to us for our sin, and that he was "made a curse for us" (Gal 3:13). As to the realities of the atonement, we shall speak in what follows of Christ's suffering and death in his human nature, but it was Christ in his *person* who effected the necessities of our salvation. And that *person* was the sinless Son of God who, as we shall see, was impeccable not only in his person but in his human nature. The necessities of redemption, therefore, the death, the rising again, and the vindication of righteousness or the declaration of justness, are referable to the impeccable sinlessness of the Redeemer. Noting his human nature, nevertheless, and with the aspect of substitution in view, Gaffin has highlighted our Lord's identity as the last Adam and has let the focus of his thought fall on the "adamic factor" involved in the accomplishment of redemption. That being so, he concludes that "The resurrection is the salvation of Jesus as the last Adam; it is . . . the point of *his* transition

---

10. Ibid., 118.
11. Ibid., 123.
12. Ibid., 124.
13. Ibid., 116.
14. Westminster Shorter Catechism, Question 27.

from wrath to grace."[15] "Christ's resurrection [is] the redemption of the last Adam."[16] That Christ's resurrection is thus seen as *his* transition from wrath to grace establishes for Gaffin the effectiveness of the sinner's sharing in the redemption that Christ accomplished for himself by that transition. But what Christ did and achieved in his redemptive work accrued, not to what has been argued in some contemporary theologies as his own justification, but to the justification directly of those for whose benefit his redemptive mission was instituted.

The claims, and the propriety of the claims, regarding the justification of Christ, or, as Gaffin has referred to it, the "judicial or forensic" justification of Christ,[17] need to be put in historical theological perspective. But first, the relevance to our present discussion of what has been said can be underlined. The line of development we have referred to sees the individual believer's justification, adoption, and sanctification as coming to effect and being what they are because at relevant levels the believer partakes of, or shares in, the redemption, justification, adoption, and sanctification that Christ achieved for himself and by doing so achieved for those who are joined in union with him. "[W]hat characterizes the redemption of Christ holds true for the redemption of the believer. As the justification, adoption, sanctification, and glorification of the former take place by and at his resurrection, so the justification, adoption, sanctification, and glorification of the latter take place in his having been raised with Christ, that is, in his having been united with Christ as resurrected. Paul does not view the justification, adoption, sanctification, and glorification of the believer as separate, distinct acts but as different facets or aspects of the *one* act of incorporation with the resurrected Christ."[18]

The doctrinal formulation of the "justification of Christ" in the sense just indicated received an impetus from the work of Geerhardus Vos, the

---

15. Gaffin, *Resurrection and Redemption*, 116.
16. Ibid., 117.
17. Gaffin, *By Faith, not by Sight*, 84
18. Gaffin, *Resurrection and Redemption*, 130–31. The doctrinal perspectives that Gaffin has proposed have influenced numerous Reformed scholars, among them Ferguson, *The Holy Spirit*, 94–113; Garcia, "Imputation and the Christology of Union with Christ," 219–51; Tipton, "Union with Christ and Justification," 23–49. See also Tipton and Waddington, editors, *Resurrection and Eschatology*. David VanDrunen, in his important "The Two Kingdoms," 209, n.4, dissents strongly from Gaffin's "simultaneity" of justification and sanctification and argues for the preservation of the *ordo salutis* in the sense clarified in his article. See also idem 221, n.28.

first professor of biblical theology at Princeton Theological Seminary in the late nineteenth century. His work, along with that of Herman Ridderbos,[19] inspired the development of what has become popularly known and widespread in Reformed circles as a redemptive-historical orientation of doctrinal theology. In his *The Pauline Eschatology* Vos spoke of "the justification of Christ," seeing in that "the certainty and the root of the Christian's resurrection."[20] And he continues, "justification comes . . . out of the resurrection; not, be it noted, out of the spiritual resurrection of the believer himself, but out of the resurrection of Christ. . . . Christ's resurrection was the *de facto* declaration of God in regard to his being just. His quickening bears in itself the testimony of his justification. God, through suspending the forces of death operating on Him, declared that the ultimate, the supreme consequence of sin had reached its termination."[21] We shall be concerned in what follows with the meaning of the "justification of Christ" that from Vos onwards gave rise to what we have already seen as a new emphasis on Christ's resurrection as his own justification.

Ridderbos, writing in Dutch in 1966, also spoke of Christ as being "justified," adducing the statement in 1 Timothy 3:16, "justified in the Spirit," to which we shall return. But his parenthetical explanatory statement continues: "i.e. vindicated, disclosed in his true significance."[22] Ridderbos' subsequent reference to the same text and to Christ's being "justified by the Spirit" is to the following effect: "that is to say, in the sight of all declared to be right."[23] Ridderbos brings to emphasis throughout his work a redemptive-historical orientation of thought and claims that "it appears unmistakably that Paul again thinks christologically and redemptive-historically and not in terms of anthropology and the *ordo salutis*."[24] We have already indicated the dependence of recent Reformed formulations on this orientation, along with the diminution of the traditional *ordo salutis* that has followed from it.[25]

19. Ridderbos, *Paul: An Outline of His Theology.*
20. Vos, *Pauline Eschatology*, 151.
21. Idem.
22. Ridderbos, op. cit., 67.
23. Ibid., 538.
24. Ibid., 211.
25. See footnote 4 above. The *ordo salutis*, or order of salvation, refers to the order of application of the benefits of the redemption accomplished by Christ, in the acts of effectual calling, regeneration, faith and repentance, justification, sanctification, persever-

The question to be faced is that of the meaning-content of the statement, particularly as it is contained in 1 Timothy 3:16, that Christ was "justified in [or by] the Spirit." We have seen that recent invocations of the phrase have been closely associated with the doctrine and reality of the Christian believer's union with Christ. That is so in the sense that the believer's justification is understood to proceed from his union with the resurrected Christ by faith. That follows from the fact that the resurrection of Christ is understood to be his own justification, in which the believer shares.

That nexus of thought was the subject of an important exchange between Robert Godfrey and David VanDrunen on the one hand and Mark Garcia on the other in the Orthodox Presbyterian Church journal, *Ordained Servant*, in 2007. Godfrey and VanDrunen, responding to Garcia's review of their work,[26] comment on "a rather new Reformed theological approach that wants to focus all of Reformed theology on union with Christ." They continue, "Whatever the exegetical and theological merits of this approach ... it ought not to be read back into Calvin as if it were his organizing principle."[27] And VanDrunen has recently followed that negative evaluation of the new perspectives in an important paper in the *Westminster Theological Journal*.[28] But it is noteworthy that in that paper, while VanDrunen argues properly for the preservation of the *ordo salutis* and the priority of justification to sanctification, he does appear to align with the historical movement we have noted on the matter of the justification of Christ. He observes that "Christ has satisfied the claims of justice and therefore *has been justified in his resurrection.*"[29] The question remains as to the meaning-content of the "justification of Christ" that is thereby in view.

---

ance, and finally glorification, as those acts come to realization in individual lives under the reality of one's union with Christ.

26. As contained in various articles in *Covenant, Justification*, edited by R. Scott Clark.

27. Godfrey and VanDrunen refer to Wenger's relevant "New Perspective on Calvin."

28. VanDrunen, "The Two Kingdoms," 207–224; 209, n. 4; 216, n. 21; 221, n.28.

29. VanDrunen, ibid., 222, italics added.

A MATTER OF EXEGESIS

The text of 1 Timothy 3:16, on which the claim of the justification of Christ is frequently and substantially based, makes six statements regarding Christ. He was, it is said, (i) manifest in the flesh; (ii) justified in the Spirit; (iii) seen of angels; (iv) preached unto the Gentiles; (v) believed on in the world; and (vi) received up into glory. The claims regarding the "justification of Christ" we have referred to proceed by extracting from that nexus the "justified in [or by] the Spirit" and referring that to the resurrection of Christ. At that point the text of Romans 1:4 is adduced in support. Ridderbos makes the point and adduces the conjunction of texts as follows: "In virtue of his resurrection from the dead, Christ, 'according to the Spirit of holiness,' is declared to be the Son of God in power (Rom 1:4); he is 'justified' (i.e., vindicated, disclosed in his true significance) by the Spirit (1 Tim 3:16). It is in that new existence of the resurrection and of the Spirit that the church may now know Christ (2 Cor 5:16), and may also judge itself to be joined with him."[30] We shall return to the possible significance of Ridderbos' parenthetical phrase. Gaffin has adduced 1 Timothy 3:16 at several points, observing, for example, that "In the parallelism of 1 Timothy 3:16 Christ's justification 'in the Spirit' is correlated with his ascension 'in glory.'"[31]

It is of interest that the recent English Standard Version translates the text at the relevant phrase as "vindicated [not 'justified'] by the Spirit," and the argument has been made by other commentators that the designation "vindicated" is, in the light of doctrinal considerations we shall adduce, not only a possible and reasonable, but a preferred translation. It is apposite, however, to take note of Gaffin's counterargument. As to the internal structure of the text, he sees the six parallel lines as forming three couplets, and "in each the two lines form an antithesis of their own expressing an aspect of the contrast brought into view by the verse as a whole . . . the first two lines ['manifest in the flesh' and 'justified in the Spirit'] form a contrast: Christ's manifestation ἐν σαρκί is set over against his justification ἐν πνεύματι."[32] Gaffin's orientation of thought at that point is not new. Newport White, in his commentary on 1 Timothy in *The Expositor's Greek Testament*, observes that "Ellicott points out that in

---

30. Ridderbos, op. cit., 67.
31. Gaffin, *Resurrection and Redemption*, 68.
32. Ibid., 119.

the three pairs of clauses the first member of each group points to *earthly* relations, the second to *heavenly*."³³ Gaffin comments that "some hold that the second line refers to Christ's vindication by endowment with the Holy Spirit during his earthly ministry . . . Recent interpretation has increasingly maintained that the basic pattern is humiliation-exaltation with the second line referring primarily to the resurrection."³⁴ And Gaffin adopts, and bases his system of thought on, the latter interpretation. "The second line, then, affirms that Christ's exaltation in the realm of the Spirit, the heavenly order, the new age, is his justification or vindication. . . . the resurrection is . . . regarded implicitly as Christ's justification or the point of entering into a state of being justified. . . . so that the translation 'vindicated,' if adopted to eliminate the usual forensic, declarative meaning, is wrong."³⁵ Thus we are back to Gaffin's conception of the "judicial or forensic significance [of] Christ's own resurrection."³⁶

An alternative reading of the six clauses contained in 1 Timothy 3:16 can, however, be suggested. They can be seen as descriptive, sequentially, of aspects of the experience of the Son of God, the Second Person of the Godhead, in his coming into the world, assuming our human nature into union with his divine nature, yet without sin, discharging the obligations and responsibilities of his messianic-redemptive assignment, and ascending again to his session at the right hand of the Father. A plain reading of the text, accordingly, suggests that the first two phrases of 1 Timothy 3:16 both refer to aspects of our Lord's appearance and experience in this world. The claim we have already looked at, that the second phrase necessarily refers primarily or only to Christ's resurrection and ascension, might therefore be quite gratuitous. If that is so, then the interpretive superstructure that lends support to the claim of the justification of Christ, in the sense we have inspected, falls to the ground.

The textual statement that God in Christ was "manifest in the flesh" refers without controversy to the incarnation of our Lord. As in John 1:14, "the Word was made flesh." That in itself is part of "the mystery of godliness," the mystery that will engage the mind throughout the rolling ages of eternity. It is the mystery that he who created time should have entered

---

33. White, *Commentary*, in Nicoll, editor, *Expositor's Greek Testament*, vol. 4, 119.
34. Gaffin, *Resurrection and Redemption*, 120.
35. Ibid., 121.
36. Gaffin, *By Faith, Not by Sight*, 84.

into and made himself subject to the passing of the time that he had created as the mode of finite existence. The second statement in the text, it can be said, the statement that Christ was "justified in the Spirit," directs our attention to the Holy Spirit's attestation to the righteousness of Christ at several times. A case in point is "the Spirit of God descending like a dove, and lighting upon him; And lo a voice from heaven, saying, This is my beloved Son, in whom I am well pleased" (Matt 3:16–17). The same testimony of the Spirit is recorded on the occasion of the transfiguration of Christ (Matt 17:5; Luke 9:35). Who is to say that the same declaration of the Spirit might not have been heard at other times during our Lord's sinless years in this world? That statement and question in no sense diminish the fact, or the importance of the fact, that at his resurrection our Lord was again declared to be righteous, and that, moreover, he was "declared to be the Son of God *with power*" (Rom 1:4).

Charles Hodge comments on the 1 Timothy text in his well-known and influential *Systematic Theology*, and observes as follows on the statement that he was "justified in the Spirit." "He . . . the Theanthropos, was justified, i.e., proved to be just, i.e., to be what he claimed to be (namely, the Son of God), by the Spirit, either by the divine nature or majesty dwelling in him, or by the Holy Ghost, whose office it is to take the things of Christ and reveal them unto us."[37] By certain testimonies of the Holy Spirit, that is, Christ was declared to be what he always was, that is "just," or necessarily and inherently righteous. There is no necessity, in the clear sense of Hodge's statement, that such a declaration was suspended only on Christ's resurrection.

But when that is said, it remains to be asked what, more precisely, is to be understood as involved in the last-mentioned and resurrection acknowledgment of Christ's righteousness. Are we to say that the acknowledgment at that point was itself "judicial-forensic" in the sense, as has been seen, that the resurrection stands as Christ's own redemption and his justification? Or again, what meaning exists in the supposition that Christ did himself stand in need of redemption and justification? A number of deeper doctrinal-theological issues bear, it would seem, on our answers to those questions. Recalling Ridderbos' parenthesis, "vindicated, disclosed in his true significance,"[38] are we not more properly to say that

---

37. Hodge, *Systematic Theology*, vol. 2, 385.
38. Ridderbos, op. cit., 67.

at his resurrection Christ was acknowledged and declared to be what he always was, the righteous Son of God who had, in the righteousness of his active and passive obedience, fulfilled impeccably all the demands of his messianic-mediatorial assignment?

TWO DOCTRINAL CONSIDERATIONS

We return to VanDrunen's summary statement that "Christ has satisfied the claims of justice and therefore has been justified."[39] What we are about to say in no sense diminishes the fact, and the importance of the fact, that in his substitutionary work on our behalf Christ satisfied all of the claims of God's justice against us. The respect in which that is so is clear on the surface of every gospel statement and does not call for rehearsal at length. The first half of VanDrunen's summary is unquestionably true. It is the meaning and import of the second half that is in question. What, again, does it mean to say that Christ was justified? For if, as Gaffin, for example, has claimed, the believer's justification is what it is because he shares in the justification that Christ accomplished for himself, there is presumably an accordance, a correspondence or likeness, between the connotation of the believer's justification and that of Christ himself. But what, we are asking, are the adequate grounds for arguing that that is so? The answer to our question requires a closer look at what, in fact, is to be held regarding the very Person of Christ and its relevance to the issue of justification. Our answer on that level requires, further, a meditation on what has been referred to doctrinally as the impeccability of Christ.

THE PERSON AND IMPECCABILITY OF CHRIST

We leave unsaid at any length at this time the description of the personhood of our Lord as that was crystallized in the Christological settlement at the Council of Chalcedon in 451 AD. The "mystery of godliness" again rests in the reality that the Second Person of the Godhead came into this world and took into union with his divine nature a human nature, "a true body and a reasonable soul,"[40] yet without sin. The union of natures that was thereby established was, as Chalcedon stated it, "without confusion, without change, without division, and without separation." Those defining characteristics mean that there was no communication of properties

---

39. VanDrunen, "The Two Kingdoms," 222.
40. Westminster Shorter Catechism, Question 22.

between the two natures. Whatever is to be said as to the *communicatio idiomatum* in relation to the personhood of Christ is to be said of the communication of properties to his person, not of any communication of properties between the respective divine and human natures. At the incarnation of our Lord, that is, there was, as Van Til has expressively put it, "no commingling of the eternal and the temporal."[41] We must go on to say that while our Lord possessed a full human nature, with all of the faculties of soul that connote human nature, in him that human nature was not personalized. Christ was not, that is to say, a human person. He was not a divine-human person, such that the two natures were combined in some sense that would render it impossible to say that he was either uniquely divine or uniquely human. Christ was, as our doctrine demands it is necessary to maintain, a divine Person.[42] It is true that Christ was not monophysite (having only one nature) and not monothelite (having only one will). There was in him a divine mind and a human mind, a divine will and a human will. We bow before the mystery.

But we take further account of our Lord's human nature. In that, he was "holy, harmless, undefiled" (Heb 7:26), and when the tempter approached it was possible for our Lord to say that "the prince of this world cometh and hath nothing in me" (John 14:30). There was not within him, given his personhood, any innate capacity to sin or disposition to sin to which the tempter could appeal. But though it is mystery again, it was in our Lord's human nature that he kept the law of God on our behalf, it was in his human nature that he suffered, and it was in his human nature that he died. We note, in making that statement, that it is not said that it was simply or only his human nature that suffered. It was Christ in his Person who suffered in his human nature. That being true, it is understandable that lying behind the claims regarding the justification of Christ that we have inspected might well be the notion of the recognition of the righteousness performed by and in that human nature; and that by virtue of the impeccable performance of the human nature the person who was in possession of it deserved, and was duly accorded, meritorious recognition or "justification." It was in his human nature that Christ rose again from the dead, and it was in his human nature that he merited the reward for his righteousness in that he was raised to the right hand of the Father. It

---

41. See Van Til, *Defense of the Faith*, 16–17.

42. Berkhof, in *Systematic Theology*, 321–22, observed that "the Logos assumed a human nature that was not personalized, that did not exist by itself."

was "when he had by himself purged our sins [in his human nature], [he] sat down at the right hand of the Majesty on high" (Heb 1:3).

But while that is so, it remains the (mysterious) case as we have just emphasized that it was the *Person* of our Lord who, in his obedience and suffering and death accomplished salvation for us. To revert to our question at the beginning, it is the *Person* of Christ who is the object of our saving faith. What was properly attributable to his human nature was, in the very nature of the case, attributable to his Person. In short, then, the question presses as to what is to be said of this *Person* of Christ who might conceivably have stood in need of, as it has been claimed, redemption and justification. The very thought of the necessity of the redemption of Christ may repel. Could such a divine Person, whatever his redemptive assignment and whatever the *modus operandi* of its accomplishment, stand in need of redemption? To claim that such necessities might be properly assigned to him by reason of his human nature is to overlook the realities that the possession of human nature connoted. For whatever questions are asked as to the outcome and meaning of the redemption he accomplished are to be asked with relation to his Person.

But that conclusion makes it necessary to bring into focus the final characteristic of the personhood of our Lord as he was in this world and as he proceeded to discharge his messianic-mediatorial undertaking on our behalf. It is necessary to say, and it is necessary to bring its relevance to bear on the entire matter of the "justification of Christ," that in his Person when he was in this world he was *impeccable*. That means, quite simply, that it was impossible for him to sin. The impeccability of Christ has long been held as the doctrine of the Reformed churches, but the formulation of its meaning has been the source of some differences of view, such, for example, as that between Charles Hodge and Robert Dabney in the nineteenth century.[43] Dabney observes that "The old doctrine of the Reformed Churches asserted not only the actual sinlessness, which none but infidels impugn, but the impeccability of our Redeemer."[44]

In assessing the impeccability of Christ, interest might fall primarily and precisely on the capacities of his human nature. It might be said, that is, that his human nature, considered in and of itself as a truly operative and responsible human nature, was capable of sin. But along with that

43. See Dabney, *Lectures*, 470–73.
44. Ibid., 470.

might be joined the statement that the human nature was not, and could not in any sense be considered as, a separable or separably responsible human nature, and that, therefore, when it was joined in union with the divine nature in the divine Person it was that divine Person who was impeccable or incapable of sin. In that way, impeccability is attributable to the Person of Christ, given that the divine nature necessarily supervised, protected, and determined the action-scope of the human nature. Dabney observes that "It is impossible that the person constituted in union with the eternal and immutable Word, can sin; for this union is an absolute shield to the lower [human] nature, against error. . . . this lower [human] nature, upon its union with the Word, was imbued with the full influences of the Holy Ghost."[45] But any argument that focuses on the ability of a human nature considered in and of itself to sin would appear to concede to Christ the *posse non peccare* (possible not to sin) but to deny to him, at least as to his humanity, the *non posse peccare* (not possible to sin).

To follow Dabney again for a moment, it is not possible to imagine that any would say "that the second Person, as eternal Word, was, or is, peccable."[46] But further, it is recalled, as already stated, that "the human nature never had its separate personality [and] never existed, and never will exist for an instant, save in personal union with the Word."[47] Therefore, since only a *person* can sin, and since the humanity that characterized our Lord was never, and could never be, alone, the question of whether the human nature, *if it had been alone*, could sin is irrelevant.

Christ, then, in his personhood was impeccable, incapable of sin. Dabney summarizes: "If this endowment of Christ's person rose no higher than a *posse non peccare* [possible not to sin], it seems obvious that there was a possibility of the failure of God's whole counsel of redemption. For, as all agree, a sinning sacrifice and intercessor could redeem no one. There must have been then, at least a decretive necessity, that all his actions should be infallibly holy."[48] We shall return to the point in connection with a comment on an argument advanced by Charles Hodge.

---

45. Ibid., 471.
46. Idem.
47. Idem.
48. Idem.

A PRELIMINARY CONCLUSION

It follows that in doctrinal construction at this time the focus of thought might more profitably fall, not on the question of "the justification of Christ," but on the manner of the accomplishment of the redemption that Christ came to provide. It is a misstep in Reformed theology, we suggest, to argue for Christ's own personal redemption, justification, adoption, and sanctification. For in the context of any such undertaking the question must come to prominence as to what meaning-content can be discovered in any such statement. Christ was "made to be sin for us" (2 Cor 5:21). But he was not constituted a sinner.

The problem consists in finding or articulating any sustainable accordance between the redemption that Christ might be deemed to have accomplished for himself, on the one hand, and the redemption of sinners on the other. For redemption means, by the very connotation of the word, redemption from the entailment of sin. But we have seen, not only that the redeemer of God's elect was himself without sin, but that it was in fact impossible for him to sin. No aspect of the categories of redemption, therefore, as they are addressed to the beneficiaries of redemption, can be attributable to him. It is not possible to claim a meaningful accordance between the necessities or fact of the sinner's redemption and the redemption that Christ might be supposed to have accomplished for himself.

What, further, of justification? It is helpful to observe that the essential meaning of "just" is that a person is just in the sight of God in that his relation to the law of God is what it ought to be. It was because sinners were disabled from ever, on their own account, being able to ascend to such a state that the sinless Son of God came to do for them what they were unable to do for themselves. In fact, by reason of the substitutionary obedience of Christ, God now looks on the beneficiaries of Christ's work as though they had themselves fulfilled all of the demands of his law. Moreover, by reason that Christ paid on their behalf the penalty due to them for their having broken the law, God now looks on them as though they had themselves paid the penalty. That is what is involved in the remarkable reality of the reciprocal imputation that occurred in and at the moment of redemption. The guilt of the sinner's sin was imputed to Christ, and the righteousness of Christ, the righteousness of his active and passive obedience, was imputed to the sinner. But as has by now been adequately established, the redeemer who came did himself at all times stand in that necessary relation to the law of God, or, to repeat the formula, his relation to the law of God "was what it ought to be." And given his divine identity there was no possibility that he could have deviated from that lawful position. He could not, therefore, *achieve* the status of "justness," precisely because he was already and always just, and the status of "justness" was always and necessarily attributable to him in his incarnate state. In short again, our Lord, in his human nature, was *just* in his fully keeping the law on our behalf, and in his active obedience he fully discharged the obligations under the covenant of works for which we were liable but which, by reason of our disabilities in sin, we were unable to discharge for ourselves.

We can recall again Ridderbos' parenthesis. He stated that the possible meaning of the statement that Christ was justified at his resurrection is simply that he was "vindicated, disclosed in his true significance." In other words, at the resurrection the Person of our Lord and the nature of his righteousness were recognized and stated to be what they always were. But that means and implies that the understanding of the Christian believer's redemption, justification, and adoption needs to rest on issues other than that of his participation in, or imputation of, the redemption, adoption, and justification that Christ accomplished for himself. Theological construction is thrown back, that is, on the *ordo salutis* construction of the meaning, not only of the accomplishment of redemption that Christ provided, but on the separate acts and works of the Holy Spirit in applying the benefits of that redemption to the sinners who are, by God's eternal decree, the beneficiaries of it.

FURTHER DOCTRINAL CONSIDERATIONS

The claims regarding the death and resurrection Christ that we have addressed are to be evaluated, we have seen, against the reality of the impeccability of Christ. The question of Christ's impeccability engaged more discussion among the nineteenth-century theologians that it has in more recent times, and even a brief review establishes its earlier currency. That Christ in his divine nature could have sinned is not worthy of argument. But at issue is the question of whether he was capable of sin in his human nature and whether, therefore, any sense exists in which he was capable of sin in his person. For it must be remembered that all of the acts of Christ, either those uniquely attributable to his divine nature or those uniquely attributable to his human nature, are properly understandable as acts of his person.

Jonathan Edwards, writing in the eighteenth century, insisted on the impeccability of Christ, meaning by that explicitly his impeccability in his human nature. His discussion is contained in the section of his treatise on *The Freedom of the Will* titled "The acts of the will of the human soul of Jesus Christ necessarily holy, yet truly virtuous, praiseworthy, rewardable, etc."[49] Edwards comments as follows on "the moral conduct and practices of our Lord Jesus Christ, which he exhibited in his human nature here in his state of humiliation. . . . his holy behaviour was necessary . . . it was impossible it should be otherwise . . . It was impossible that the acts of the will *of the human soul* of Christ should, in any instance, degree, or circumstance, be otherwise than holy, and agreeable to God's nature and will."[50] Christ, as to both his human and his divine natures, was impeccable. Edwards' ensuing discussion is worthy of close inspection.

The late nineteenth-century Reformed theologian at Union Seminary, New York, W. G. T. Shedd, addresses the doctrine of Christ's impeccability at length.[51] Again he concludes that Christ "was characterized not only by the posse non peccare, but by the non posse peccare."[52] The angels who fell were originally holy but were not impeccable. So Adam in his initial state was holy, intrinsically holy and not poised in a state of moral neutrality, but he was defectible, mutable, and not impeccable. But "The case of Jesus Christ, the second Adam, was different, in that he was not only able to resist temptation, but it was infallibly certain that he would resist it."[53] And Shedd goes on to examine Scripture proofs of our Lord's impeccability.

Shedd's argument is worthy of further note. He acknowledged that "The divine nature is both intemptable, and impeccable. 'God cannot be tempted with evil,' James 1:13. 'It is impossible for God to lie,' Hebrews 6:18. The human nature, on the contrary, is both temptable and peccable. [But] [w]hen these two natures are *united* in one theanthropic person, as they are in the incarnation, the divine determines and controls the human, not

---

49. Edwards, *Freedom of the Will*, Morgan, PA edition, 156.
50. Ibid., 156–57, italics added.
51. Shedd, *Dogmatic Theology*, vol. 2, 330–49.
52. Ibid., 330.
53. Idem.

the human the divine."⁵⁴ Shedd had previously stated that "It is the divine nature, not the human nature, which is the base of Christ's person."⁵⁵ So that, as Shedd sees it, "Christ, while having a peccable human *nature* in his constitution, was an impeccable *person*."⁵⁶ Further, "the divine nature constantly supports the human nature under all the temptations to sin that are presented to it . . . . [but] It deserts the humanity so that it may suffer for the *atonement* of sin, but it never deserts the humanity so that it may *fall into sin itself*."⁵⁷ But, contrary to Shedd's conclusion at this point, it can be argued that our Lord's human nature was in itself impeccable.

Shedd's construction at this point can be set against that of Dabney that we noted earlier. Dabney concluded, we recall, that since only a *person* can sin, and since the humanity that characterized our Lord was never, and could never be, alone, the question of whether the human nature, *if it had been alone*, could sin is irrelevant. Again, the fuller arguments of both Dabney and Shedd are worthy of close inspection, both concluding, in one way or another, on the impeccability of Christ.

We noted earlier also, that Dabney had dissented from the view of Christ's impeccability that had been addressed by Charles Hodge. It is remarkable that Hodge held a view on this important question from which, by implication, the arguments I have already given dissent. Hodge rightly observes that "A sinful Saviour from sin is an impossibility. He could not have access to God. He could not be a sacrifice for sins; and He could not be the source of holiness and eternal life to his people."⁵⁸ But Hodge goes on to say that "This sinlessness of our Lord, however, does not amount to absolute impeccability. It was not a *non potest peccare*. If He was a true man He must have been capable of sinning. . . . If from the constitution of his person it was impossible for Christ to sin, then his temptation was unreal and without effect, and He cannot sympathize with his people."⁵⁹ Such a conclusion from the illustrious Hodge, eminent among the nineteenth-century Princeton custodians of the Reformed faith, may well be surprising.

---

54. Ibid., 332.
55. Ibid., 269.
56. Ibid., 333.
57. Ibid., 335, italics added.
58. Charles Hodge, *Systematic Theology*, vol. 2, 457.
59. Idem.

It is understandable, of course, that the question should arise as to whether, because our Lord was impeccable in his human nature, the temptations to which he was exposed were "real," and whether he did, in fact, actually realize the spiritual assaults of temptation in his victory over them. And does, therefore, a true accordance exist between his temptations and those to which the Christian is subject? For the letter to the Hebrews has stated that he "was in all points tempted like as we are" (Heb 4:15). To resolve such a question it is necessary to distinguish between, first, the natural act of the human intellect in recognizing the possible attractiveness of a given, and in the present case, forbidden, object, and secondly, a natural impulse to the embrace of it. Dabney observes in that connection that "While the *human will* of Jesus was rendered absolutely incapable of concupiscence by the indwelling of the Godhead *and its own natural endowment*; He could doubtless represent to Himself mentally precisely how a sinful object affects both the mind and heart of His imperfect people. Does this not fit Him to feel for and to succor them?"[60] In the presence of temptation the human will of our Lord was perfectly free. But that will was completely and perfectly holy, such that the mental recognition of evil in temptation could not, and did not, conduce to any appetitive desire for the evil that the tempter brought before him. In that respect the second Adam differed from the first. In his possession of free will our first parent was nevertheless mutable in soul. In the second Adam his dispositions to holiness were perfectly and immutably holy. It was infallibly certain that he would not choose to sin.

For purposes of our present study, the relevance of what has been said is that the impeccability of Christ, as to his person and as to both his divine and human natures, renders irrelevant the arguments we have noted regarding the purported fact of, and the necessity of, his own redemption and justification at and by his resurrection.

A final question calls for brief comment. It was noted that when Gaffin, for example, allowed the focus of his thought to fall on Christ's resurrection he virtually subordinated all other aspects of soteriology to that perspective. In doing so he diminished, virtually to the point of irrelevance, what has been historically and traditionally understood in Reformed theology as the *ordo salutis*, or the order of application of redemption to those for whom Christ died. His emphasis, following from

---

60. Dabney, *Lectures*, 472, italics added.

his dependence on the redemptive-historical orientation of thought, is on the *historia salutis*, rather than, as in historic Reformed theology, the *ordo salutis*. Gaffin has aligned his work with that of Ridderbos, who "in a variety of contexts ... underscore[s] that the apostle's interest is the former (i.e., redemptive-historical) rather than the latter (i.e., in terms of the *ordo salutis*)."[61] As to the focus of Paul's soteriology, Gaffin insists, "we need to keep in mind that his controlling focus is the *historia salutis*, not the *ordo salutis*," and Gaffin there acknowledges that he adopts "a perspective that represents something of a difference in accent from what has largely been true beginning with the Reformation."[62]

The terms of the *ordo salutis* will be well-known, as John Murray, for example, has treated them in his *Redemption—Accomplished and Applied*.[63] When Gaffin argued that "union with the resurrected Christ by faith is the central motif of Paul's applied soteriology,"[64] he concluded, we have seen, that "the justification, adoption, sanctification, and glorification [of the believer] take place in his having been raised with Christ ... This means ... that Paul does not view justification, adoption, sanctification, and glorification of the believer as separate, distinct acts but as different facets or aspects of the *one* act of incorporation with the resurrected Christ."[65] In that, it is to be feared, we have a diminution of the fact and the salvific effect of the redemptive office of the Holy Spirit. What the *ordo salutis* conception understands as separable acts of the Holy Spirit, that is to say, Gaffin understands as simultaneous and as referable to the import for the believer of his union by faith with the resurrected Christ. He drives home his point. He sees an "insoluble difficulty" in the *ordo salutis* in its "trying to explain how these acts are related to the act of being joined *existentially* to Christ. If at the point of inception this union is prior ... what need is there for the other acts?"[66] "Paul does not view the justification of the sinner (the imputation of Christ's righteousness) as an act having a discrete structure of its own."[67]

61. Gaffin, *Resurrection and Redemption*, 14.
62. Gaffin, *By Faith, Not By Sight*, 24.
63. Murray, *Redemption—Accomplished and Applied*.
64. Gaffin, *Resurrection and Redemption*, 132.
65. Ibid., 130–31.
66. Ibid., 138–39.
67. Ibid., 132.

Our dissent is from such a surrender of the *ordo salutis*. We have noted that a strenuous counterargument and insistence on both the *ordo salutis* in its hitherto established sense and the priority of justification to sanctification has been made by David VanDrunen.[68] It is beyond the scope of our present purpose to explore the issue further in the following important respect. But we repeat, the diminution of the *ordo salutis* in the manner that certain contemporary theologies have proposed is in serious danger of diminishing the doctrine and fact of the redemptive office of the Holy Spirit. It diminishes his work in applying the benefits of Christ's redemption to the souls of those whom he calls to Christ. At issue, in even broader terms, is the unity of purpose in the divine distribution of redemptive offices among the Persons of the Godhead and the total divine *modus operandi* of redemption.

A significant recent work that dissents from the traditional *ordo salutis* is that of Michael Horton.[69] In his dissent from earlier Reformed formulations Horton relates his argument to the priority given in certain contemporary theologies to the believer's union with Christ. Of the importance of that union, of course, and its place in Reformed theology, there can be no doubt. The importance and significance of that union is acknowledged in Murray's comments that union with Christ is "a very broad and embracive subject. . . . [I]n its broader aspects it underlies every step of the application of redemption."[70] But Horton's argument is influenced by his particular construction of the place and meaning of the act of justification. He writes in apparent agreement with the claim that "regeneration . . . flows from justification as its consequence."[71] He states that the "initiating moment of new life [regeneration] . . . is the result of the justifying verdict that one receives through faith."[72]

That construction, in the context of Horton's attempt to effect a paradigm shift in Reformed theology, is justified, as he sees it, by what he imports from contemporary speech-act theory. In his discussion of "Speech-act theory and effectual calling," he concludes on that basis that "regeneration is not a direct and immediate act of God on the soul, but the perlocutionary

---

68. VanDrunen, "The Two Kingdoms."

69. Horton, *Covenant and Salvation*. See the discussion of Horton's arguments in Vickers, *When God Converts a Sinner*, chapter 7.

70. Murray, *Redemption*, 201. The doctrine of the believer's union with Christ is discussed more fully in Vickers, *When God Converts a Sinner*, chapter 7.

71. Horton, op. cit., 202.

72. Ibid., 204.

effect of the illocutionary act pronounced by the Father in the Son through the Spirit."[73] (Horton's terminological inventions are defined in the footnote at this point). In Horton's thought system he is leaving a wide opening for the Holy Spirit to apply to the human soul the meaning of what God has said. That applicatory, or perlocutionary, work of the Spirit is, in Horton's view, what is involved in, or amounts to, the regeneration of the sinner. In that way, Horton sees the perlocutionary work of regeneration following as a result of, and not as preceding, God's spoken act of justification. That, it is clear, is a deliberate inversion of the Reformed doctrine of the *ordo salutis* as it has been historically understood.

Our immediate interest is in the respects in which the diminution of the *ordo salutis* does, as we have said, endanger the doctrine of the work of the Holy Spirit. Given that, the question of the Spirit's work in regeneration would not seem to be clearly preserved in Horton's formulation. Regeneration, to the contrary, by reason of the endowments it conveys to the faculties of the soul, establishes the gift of faith as a capacity of exercise at the same time as it renews the soul in its union with Christ.[74] When, then, that newly endowed capacity of faith is exercised, the divine declarative act of justification follows. But when the *ordo salutis*, the application of redemption, is then followed out in corresponding terms, the validity and usefulness of the Reformed construction, as Berkhof, for example, has seen it, become clear. Berkhof observes that "Even the very first blessing of the saving grace of God which we receive already presupposes a union with the Person of the Mediator."[75] He goes on to distinguish between God's work in the establishment of the union, the *unio mystica*, which "is effected by the Holy Spirit in a mysterious and supernatural way,"[76]

73. Ibid., 220, 230. See Vickers, *When God Converts a Sinner*, chapter 7. In the terminology of speech-act theory an illocutionary act refers to what it is the speaker intends to convey by a statement he makes. It refers to the message, such as the intent to inform or persuade, for example, that the speaker sets out to communicate. The understanding of the statement in the mind of the hearer, on the other hand, or the "uptake" by the hearer, or what it is that actually functions in the hearer as the standard by which the meaning of what is said is to be measured and perhaps acted upon, is referred to as the perlocutionary response.

74. That endowment of the faculties with new abilities and capacities and the creation of a new *habitus* in the soul do not necessarily raise the error of a participationist ontology from which Horton rightly dissents. Nor does it point to a "schizophrenic ontology" as Horton fears. See Horton, op. cit., 216.

75. Berkhof, *Systematic Theology*, 447.

76. Idem.

and the believer's "subjective realization" of the union.⁷⁷ Noting the possible time differences involved, Berkhof concludes that "union with Him [Christ] logically precedes both regeneration and justification by faith, while yet, chronologically, the moment we are united with Christ is also the moment of our regeneration and justification." But Berkhof observes that the temporal relationship is further explained by the "reciprocal action" that is involved. "The initial act is that of Christ, who unites believers to himself by regenerating them and thus producing faith in them. On the other hand, the believer also unites himself to Christ by a conscious act of faith, and continues the union, under the influence of the Holy Spirit, by the constant exercise of faith."⁷⁸

We note Berkhof's judicious separation of Christ's "*producing* faith" in the believer and the believer's "*act*" or "*exercise*" of faith. In short, as Berkhof concludes on this important relationship and "the mediation of the mystical union," "While the union is effected when the sinner is renewed by the operation of the Holy Spirit, he does not become cognizant of it and does not actively cultivate it until the conscious operation of faith begins."⁷⁹ Addressing "the subjective realization of the mystical union," Berkhof concludes that though we are joined to Christ as the branches are to the vine, "it is not correct to say that the mystical union is the fruit of man's believing acceptance of Christ."⁸⁰ For "Faith . . . a gift of God . . . enables us to appropriate on our part what is given unto us in Christ, and to enter ever-increasingly into conscious enjoyment of the blessed union with Christ, which is the source of all our spiritual riches."⁸¹ The union with Christ of which we have spoken is not the result of faith in Christ; it is the reality from which faith in Christ emanates.

CONCLUSION

Our conclusion, then, is threefold. First, we conclude that what we have seen as the modern attempt to reform Reformed theology, particularly on the level of soteriology, by speaking of the redemption and justification of Christ is a misstep. Second, when the doctrine of the Person of Christ

---

77. Ibid., 450.
78. Idem.
79. Ibid., 452.
80. Ibid., 449.
81. Idem.

is brought to bear on the questions at hand, the impeccability of Christ in both his human nature and his divine personhood must be brought to emphasis. And third, we dissent from the attempts to diminish the meaning and doctrinal relevance of the *ordo salutis* and, in connection with that particularly, the work of the Holy Spirit in the application of redemption.

Reformed theology does not stand in need of the paradigm changes that certain modern theologies have proposed.

8

Adoption and the Paradox of Faith

MY OBJECTIVE IN THIS chapter is to raise a number of issues that have to do directly with the meaning and conduct of the Christian life. In doing that I shall direct attention to three propositions that bear heavily on Christian belief, intending thereby to draw out the significance for Christian living of aspects of discussion in the preceding chapters. Taken together, the propositions I shall suggest address the status to which the Christian believer has been raised and the prospects for his life in this world. In stating the propositions I shall raise two rather fundamental questions. First, what is it in which salvation is grounded and what is the *modus operandi* of it? And second, to what extent is it possible for us to achieve in this life an understanding of what that salvation means and involves? It might be supposed at the beginning that of course we know what salvation is and means; and of course we know what is to be known about it. But such a claim, I suggest, is at best superficial and evidences a failure to be concerned with the depth of meaning and reflection that the questions before us hold and deserve.

I shall be bringing into focus two issues that deserve our deepest reflection. And in order to exhibit the issues clearly I shall adduce in due course a question of textual exegesis that bears directly on them. But first, let me observe the following by way of orientation. When we address the fact and the process of our salvation we are speaking of the question of *soteriology*; and when we speak of the possibility of the knowledge of what salvation involves we are raising the question of *epistemology*. I am therefore bringing into focus the closely related questions of *soteriology* and *epistemology* because it is necessary to see the manner in which both those questions are resolved, so far as their bearing on the Christian life is concerned. And at that point an important conclusion is to be held by the Christian mind. It is that both those questions are resolved in, and by,

Christ. If we do not see that the questions of both salvation and the possibility of knowledge find their resolution in Christ, we have decided to be content with a form of belief that is lower than what the biblical revelation provides. Let me state and then summarize my three propositions.

The *first proposition* is in two parts. First, by reason of the regenerating work of the Spirit of God in the soul the believer is joined to Christ in a vital and indissoluble union. He is, at the moment of faith, the beneficiary of God's declarative-forensic statements of justification and adoption. But second, the believer nevertheless *does not know* in this life, and in the nature of the divine-human relation he *cannot know* in this life, all that is meant and implied by that union and adoption.

The *second proposition* follows and states that the capacity to know, in the sense of understanding the complete implications of the facts at issue, is restricted by the finitude that determines the human epistemic capacity. That is to say, as we shall see more fully, because man is the analogue of God his Creator both as to his being and his knowledge, while he can know *truly* what God has declared, he cannot know *comprehensively* anything of God's declaration and purpose. His knowledge is necessarily partial. That partialness, moreover, is further restricted or is aggravated by the fact of man's naturally sinful state, from the entailment of which he cannot escape completely in this life. The reality of sin and its clinging residue in the life of the Christian implies that he is necessarily unaware of its magnitude, its gravity, and its degree of discordance from the purity of life to which the Christian is called.

My third proposition follows as a resolution of the realities implicit in what has already been said. We are now interested in the *soteriological aspects* and the *epistemological aspects* of what God has said and done in setting forth a salvation for sinners. The *third proposition,* then, is that *It is in Christ that both the soteriological and the epistemological problems are solved.* Our objective is to accord all honor to Christ in whom, as the apostle stated to the Colossian church, "are hid all the treasures of wisdom and knowledge" (Col 2:3). In Christ we find the way of salvation. And in him we find all necessary categories of meaning and criteria of explanation.

Let me introduce my argument further by referring again briefly to the natural state of man as he exists after, and as a result of, Adam's fall. I have spoken at greater length in the preceding chapters of the fact that man was created as the image of God, and that following his fall in Adam

Adoption and the Paradox of Faith

he remains the image of God.[1] Leaving aside for the present a fuller statement regarding the faculties of the soul in their primeval status and relations, it can be said on the basis of the biblical data that at the fall all of the faculties of the soul were depraved. That was so in the sense that they were deprived of their initial abilities and capacities and man was, as a result, disabled from discharging the obligations of the covenant of creation, or his offices as prophet, priest, and king. But it is important to hold in view for our present purposes that at the fall the faculties were not obliterated. After his fall into the state of sin man was still capable of expressing the emotion of affection. His affective faculty, as a sheer capability of exercise, remains. Similarly, his intellectual faculty was not obliterated and he was still able to think. And his volitional faculty similarly remained, in that he was able to will and to implement action based on his will. Of course it is to be said also that the actions of all of the faculties were henceforth subject to a bias that sin had introduced into the soul. That bias meant that the intellectual faculty was now deprived of the ability to know God truly, the emotional faculty was such that man naturally hated God, and the will was bound and unable to act in accordance with the law of God.

But because the intellectual faculty remains as the natural ability to think, God says to the sinner, "Come now, and let us reason together" (Isa 1:18). And while it is true that in man's natural state "the god of this world hath blinded the minds of them which believe not" (2 Cor 4:4), our Lord himself, at the very beginning of his ministry called on the sinner to think. For Christ "began to preach, and to say, Repent" (Matt 4:17). And "repent" means, in its basic connotation, "think again." What is the Christian life, then, apart from a being "transformed by the renewing of your mind" (Rom 12:2)? And it is an aspect of the high status of the Christian person that he has "the mind of Christ" (1 Cor 2:16).[2] While the import of that last statement is that now, as a result of the ministry of the Spirit of Christ, the born-again person begins to see all things as Christ sees them, it is true that the imperfections and partialness of seeing and knowing of which we have already spoken necessarily remain.

Our propositions, then, are as follows: *First*, the Christian believer is joined to Christ in an indissoluble union though he does not yet know, and cannot know, the full meaning of that union. *Second*, in the very

---

1. See Vickers, *Christian Confession*, chapter 3.
2. See the fuller discussion in chapter 6.

nature of the human condition, characterized as that is by both finitude and sin, it is impossible for one to know anything of God's revelation and purpose fully and comprehensively. *Third*, the consequent *soteriological* and *epistemological* problems are solved in Christ. We must now work out why and how that is so. We have readily available to us Scriptural data that bear directly on the implications of those propositions.

A QUESTION OF EXEGESIS

An unsettled question in the history of exegesis relates to God's statement recorded by the prophet Isaiah, "For my thoughts are not your thoughts, neither are your ways my ways" (Isa 55:8). We leave aside what Edward J. Young has noted as the chiastic arrangement of the text. In the preceding verse the prophet had spoken of the wicked man's "way" and "thoughts"; and now with a reversal of order he speaks of God's "thoughts" and "ways." A further chiasm is contained in the text, where reference is made to "*my* thoughts" and "*your* thoughts," followed by the reversal, "*your* ways" and "*my* ways."[3] But our immediate interest is not in literary form. The question we raise, recalling our introductory observations, is whether the statement is to be understood as carrying primarily a soteriological or an epistemological import. What, that is, are we to understand as the primary statement of the text?

Consider first its soteriological import. If the import is primarily soteriological the statement is being made that God's thoughts and ways relevant to man's salvation and the possibilities and scope of it are completely different from what man himself could have imagined or contemplated. The issue, then, is the meaning of the process of salvation and reconciliation with God. If, to take the other alternative, our focus should fall on the text's epistemological import, the statement is to the effect that God knows and thinks in a manner, on levels, and with a comprehensive awareness of all the relations involved, of which man in his finitude is incapable. The issue then is a matter of how and what we know, and of what we are able to know. The knowledge of God, the text is then saying, the knowledge that God has of himself and of all of the relations within reality external to the Godhead that he spoke into existence, is incomprehensible to us.

---

3. Young, *The Book of Isaiah*, vol. 3, 382.

Our task now, in the light of what has been said, is to address two questions. First, what relation, if any, is to be understood as existing between the two possible levels of primary import we have raised, and what might be the bearing of the one on the other in their contributions to full Christian understanding? Second, and more particularly, what light does that conjunction of imports throw on our present question of the meaning of the Christian believer's adoption into the family of God?

The soteriological emphasis of the text is clear from the surrounding context, which lays out the invitation to sinners to come and partake of the water of life, to "buy . . . without money and without price" (Isa 55:1). There we have the promise of God: "I will make an everlasting covenant . . . even the sure mercies of David" (Isa 55:1–3). In the conception of the sure mercies of David we have the messianic promise written large. Indeed, we shall see in due course that the sin that necessarily clutters the Christian life, what we shall characterize as both willful sins and sins of ignorance, is to be recognized for its relation to the "everlasting covenant" that God has established with his people in Christ. An emphasis on the soteriological import of the text is consistent with the context that Isaiah had established at the beginning of the uniquely evangelical aspect of his prophecy. That the entire way of salvation is profoundly different from what man himself could have imagined is projected in the statement that "Every valley shall be exalted, and every mountain and hill shall be made low; and the crooked shall be made straight, and the rough places plain" (Isa 40:4). In other words, in the whole matter of God's design of salvation and the rescue from sin into which Adam's fall had plunged the race, man's possible imaginations are turned completely upside down. The issue points to what the apostle Paul spoke about convincingly when he observed that here in the whole conception and process of redemption we have "the mystery of Christ" (Eph 3:4), and that "great is the mystery of godliness" (1 Tim 3:16).

But the epistemological import of the text is equally clear and important. It is in fact implicit in what has already been said. Young observes in that connection that "The purpose is to state that God possesses *thoughts* (i.e. purposes and designs) and *ways*, and that these are not to be identified with those of man."[4] The Puritan commentator Matthew Henry makes a statement in context that clearly contains elements of both the emphases

---

4. Idem. Young here follows the apologetic of Van Til as stated most comprehensively in *Defense of the Faith* and *Christian Theory of Knowledge*.

we have noted: "God's counsels [are] high and transcendent, his thoughts and ways infinitely above ours. . . . 'for,' (says he) 'my thoughts and ways are not as yours. Yours are conversant only about things beneath; they are of the earth earthy; but mine are above, *as the heaven is high above the earth*.'"[5] God knows and thinks, and man knows and thinks because he was created as the image of God. As God is rational, so his image, man, is rational. As God's revealed attributes of holiness, justice, and righteousness declare him to be a moral God, so man also is the moral image of God. But as man's being is derivative and analogical of God's being, so his thought and his epistemic capacity are analogical of the thought of God. There exists, that is to say, not only a *quantitative*, but also a *qualitative* difference between God's knowledge and man's knowledge. Man, we have said, is the analogue of God as to both his being and his knowledge. In our createdness and finitude we necessarily think sequentially, in temporal processes. But God, who created time and called it into being as the mode of our finite existence, knows and thinks outside of time, in the eternal moment of his eternal day.[6] God knows the fullness of structural interrelations between all possible objects of knowledge that, in the nature of our createdness and finitude, are inaccessible to us.

We can bring together the soteriological and the epistemological, both of which are now seen to bear on the human condition, and in doing so we are able to see that the relevant issues converge in the meaning to us of the Person and work of Christ. Two results follow for the Christian believer's understanding of what the redeeming grace of God means and implies. First, as to soteriology, the sinner who is now conscious of his rescue from sin by the salvation that God has set forth bows humbly before his Creator and Redeemer-judge and knows that his salvation is due only and completely to the incomprehensible design and grace of God. Nothing exists in the sinner's existential status, nothing could have come within the ken of his imagination, that could have conjured a way to his reconciliation with God. Such an understanding and conviction sees that all the issues of soteriology are solved in Christ.

---

5. Matthew Henry, *Commentary*, loc. cit.

6. See Augustine, *Confessions*, Book 11 on the meaning of time. Van Til has observed that "Time . . . is God-created as a mode of finite existence," *Systematic Theology*, 66. Bavinck has similarly stated that "time—intrinsic time—is a mode of existence of all created and finite beings," *Doctrine of God*, 156.

Second, as to epistemology, the Christian knows that he is dependent on God's communication to him by his Holy Spirit for his understanding on all levels, on those levels relating to his salvation and those having to do with all aspects of the meaning of his existence and the interpretation of reality. He knows that God alone has designed for him all relevant and efficient criteria of knowledge and truth on all levels of investigation and understanding. For as we have anticipated, he has now seen that in Christ "are hid all the treasures of wisdom and knowledge" (Col 2:3). The epistemological as well as the soteriological problem is solved, and it is solved for the twofold reasons that exist in and because of Christ.

That is so because, first, on the level of *soteriology*, complete salvation issues from the substitutionary life and work of Christ in this world; and secondly, on the level of *epistemology*, Christ has communicated to the Christian believer the necessary criteria of validity and truth on all levels of knowledge and comprehension. The soteriological and the epistemological now find their common root in Christ and his conveyance of truth to those whom he has redeemed. The question of Isaiah's text is resolved. It is by Christ that we are saved, and it is by him that we have true (though not comprehensive) knowledge and understanding. In Christ the valid criteria of truth that Adam lost are rediscovered to us, the efficient principles, criteria, and presuppositions of knowledge are revealed, and our journey into understanding on all levels is secure under the guidance that Christ provides to us. The Person and work of Christ and the invitation to seek blessing in him structure the context of the chapter in the prophecy of Isaiah with which we began.

THE *SUMMUM BONUM* TO KNOW GOD

What has just been said can be stated in different terms. What, we may ask, is the *summum bonum*, the highest good, for the human person whom God has established in his own image? Surely the *summum bonum* is to see God. That is precisely what is guaranteed to us in the word that has declared God's purposes. That, surely, is the culmination of what is in prospect for the redeemed in what the prophet has held before us as "the sure mercies of David." We shall see God in Christ, in his glorified humanity, in the last great day, and we shall know that we see God. What other manifestations of the Person and image of God will be available to us, what Shekinah cloud of glory or what burning bush, is at this time hidden from us. But while that *summum bonum* of seeing God is delayed until the day of his appearing in Christ, is there not, we may ask, a *summum bonum* for the Christian believer *in this life*? Is there not a highest good, the consciousness of which is itself the foretaste in this life, "the earnest of our inheritance" (Eph 1:13), the precursor, of what is to come? In this life we do not *see* God, but in the realization of our highest good we *know* God.

To say that it is possible in this life to know God is to fly in the face of what has come down to contemporary thought as the post-Kantian agnosticism that we have encountered in the preceding chapters. Kant's agnosticism, it has been seen, rests in his acknowledgment that while it is not possible to prove the existence of God, neither is it possible to prove that God does not exist. God is an assumption of Kant's practical reason, not of pure reason. Subsequent argument proceeded "as if" God existed. Theology in the post-Kantian sense has claimed with Kant that he abolished knowledge to make room for faith. But such a claim has no relation to what is to be understood as the faith in Christ that we have seen is the gift of God. What we claim, rather, is that knowledge of God is possible because God has condescended to make himself known. Both Scriptural data and Christian experience bear testimony to the fact. We say, therefore, that to know God is in this life the Christian's highest good.

But what, then, is the meaning of the statement that in this life it is possible to "know" God? We are not speaking now of a bare cognition of the existence of God. The devils have that knowledge and they tremble (Jas 2:19). But as our Lord himself declared, "[T]his is life eternal, that they might know thee the only true God." (John 17:3). We know God because God has made himself known to us in Christ.

Isaiah's prophecy has reminded us that God's thoughts are higher than our thoughts, that they are different, substantially, qualitatively, and in their manner of being, than our thoughts. But it is of the essence of the revelation of redemption that God has accommodated himself to our humanity and to our sin, in that he has disclosed his thought to us. In his condescension God has spoken to us in the language of men in order that we might know him. We have said that his thoughts, in the totality of their being and scope, are incomprehensible to us. But it is available to us to know him, and to know his thoughts in the degree that is effective to our highest good in this life and our eternal security.

But at this stage it is necessary to face the relevance of that conclusion, not only to the meaning of salvation by reason of the work of Christ, but its relevance also to the meaning of adoption into the family of God. Two things follow. First, in the same way as justification before God involves a declarative, forensic statement of God, so adoption into his family again involves his declarative, forensic statement. In short, both justification and adoption involve declarative, forensic, once-for-all statements of God. They both have a distinctly legal reference. By God's statement of justification we are declared to have satisfied all the demands of God's law, a divine judicial statement made possible by reason that the righteousness of Christ is placed to our account. Similarly, the statement of adoption is forensic in the respect that it establishes a legally irrefutable relation from which God's law of justice cannot dislodge us.

Second, again in the light of our conclusion regarding the relation between the soteriological and the epistemological, while we recognize the legalities that are thereby satisfied we acknowledge that we cannot plumb the depth of meaning of either our justification or our adoption. That is what is at issue in our present discussion. *We cannot plumb the depth of meaning of either our justification or our adoption.* In short again, we know that we have been redeemed by the design and implementation of God's covenantal grace, that we are eternally secure within the compass his covenant provides, but we do not in this life know and understand all of the meaning and scope of that redemption. At this time we "see through a glass darkly" (1 Cor 13:12). We hold a conviction of our redemption that nothing can dislodge, "neither death, nor life, nor angels, nor principalities, nor powers, nor things present, nor things to come, nor height, nor depth, nor any other creature" (Rom 8:38–39). Enlightened by the Spirit of God, we know that "now are we the sons of God, and it doth not yet appear what we shall be: but we know that, when he shall appear, we shall be like him" (1 John 3:2). *But we do not know, and we cannot know, all that in the mind and counsel of God is involved in our salvation and adoption.*

THE PARADOX OF FAITH

I have referred in the title of this chapter to the paradox of faith. A paradox is a seeming contradiction. Consider the following observations that describe where we stand as to our knowing and knowledge. We know certain things and we hold a firm conviction of the truth of what we know. We know, for example, that we are indissolubly joined to God in Christ. *But we don't know that as God knows it.* We know certain things that are true. But we don't know all the meaning of the things that are true. We don't know the meaning of all that is involved in them for this life, and certainly not all they project for the life that is to come. It seems that our knowledge is paradoxical in a sense. It seems that we know, and yet we don't know. But we reject at that point the conclusion of paradox and we reflect, rather, on the fact that our knowledge is partial. The knowledge we possess on the levels we are addressing is true, but it is incomplete. It is not, to use apologetic language, comprehensive knowledge. We await the full interpretation of the meaning content of what it is that we know. We know, moreover, that certain things that we cannot now see, and statements that God has made to us about them, are true. We know the truth of things that we cannot know in their full scope and significance. That, it may appear, is paradoxical. For how can we know that certain things are true if we cannot know their full import and meaning? But as we have argued in more than one place, comprehensiveness of knowledge is not prerequisite to truth of knowledge.

But a paradox remains. It is a paradox that informs the realities of the life of God's people as they work out the progress in righteousness to which they have been called. It rests in the fact that God has made us to be saints (1 Cor 1:2; Eph 1:1; Phil 1:1; Col 1:2), but we are nevertheless sinners. Saints and sinners. That is the paradox. How can it be said that we have union with Christ while yet it is necessary to confess that we are sinners? How can it be said that the Christian believer has been adopted into the family of God, while yet he sins? The paradox of faith consists in the life of faith to which we have been called and on which we have entered. It is a paradox of the life of faith as that is lived out in the presence of God.

We look, therefore, at some of the implications for the Christian life of what has been said. Of foremost relevance is the doctrine of adoption into the family of God and the ethical imperatives which that carries for Christian conduct and life.

ADOPTION

It would be a mistake of high order to separate in our thought two aspects of God's dealings with us in salvation that he has inseparably joined. The related doctrines of, first, the Christian believer's adoption into the family of God, and second, his union with Christ must be held in mutually reinforcing relation. In the Holy Spirit's work of regeneration in the soul the awakened sinner is established in union with Christ. The Westminster Catechism states that the Spirit applies to the sinner the benefits of Christ's redemption by "working faith in us and thereby *uniting us to Christ* in our effectual calling."[7] The Savoy Declaration of Faith refers pointedly to "[Those] that are effectually called and regenerated, *being united to Christ* . . ."[8] The Dutch Reformed theologian à Brakel observed in relation to the beneficiaries of the grace of regeneration that "Their mind, will, and affections have been changed. They have become new creatures."[9] And "when the moment of good pleasure arrives for each of the elect . . . the Holy Spirit quickens and grants him spiritual life, *this being a consequence of the soul's union with God in Christ*."[10]

We say, then, that by God's covenantal design the Holy Spirit works in the souls of those for whom Christ died to the effect that first, those persons are assumed into union with God himself in Christ; and second, by their adoption they are counted members of the family of God and entitled to all the endowments and benefits that follow from, and are associated with, that status. The reciprocal relations that exist between these two levels of benefit, adoption and union with Christ, have in turn several important implications for the Christian believer's life and walk of faith.

First, the union thus established is, as has been said, indissoluble. That indissolubility is to be variously understood. It follows not only from the fact that it has been established by the terms of God's covenantal promise, God's faithfulness to which he has sworn by an oath (Heb 6:17). It follows, with equally secure import, from the reality that as Christ himself cannot be divided, so life in union with him is, for that reason and on that ground, indivisibly established. The union, in other words, is a vital union whereby the very life of Christ is communicated to the believer by the dwelling within him of the Holy Spirit whom Christ has sent. The apostle has stated the issue clearly: "I live, yet not I, but Christ liveth in me" (Gal 2:20). By virtue of that indwelling of the Spirit the new-born person is "sealed with [the] Holy Spirit of promise," or the Holy Spirit who had

---

7. Westminster Shorter Catechism, Question 30, italics added.

8. Savoy Declaration of Faith, XIII:1, italics added. The Savoy Declaration follows the Westminster Confession of Faith very closely in most of its chapters. But in their otherwise similar chapters 13, the words "being united to Christ" are included in Savoy but omitted from Westminster.

9. à Brakel, *The Christian's Reasonable Service*, vol. 1, 183.

10. Idem, italics added.

been promised (Eph 1:13), and by the Holy Spirit that seal is "unto the day of redemption" (Eph 4:30). à Brakel has rightly observed that "This union is real, essential, true, complete, without any reservation, eternally inseparable, spiritual."[11]

Second, it follows from the Scriptural data that union with Christ involves union with the three Persons of the Godhead. Staggering as the thought and realization may be, it would be a diminution of the truth to overlook the fact that the mystical union carries with it nothing less than union with the triune Persons of the Godhead, the Father, the Son, and the Holy Spirit. The union is not one of identity. It is not an essential union, in the sense that the Christian believer partakes of the essence of the Godhead. He does, it is true, partake of the communicable attributes of God. But union with Christ does not imply the divinization of the believer. Neither will there be a divinization of the redeemed person when he sees God in Christ in the great eternal day.

Third, it follows that it is as an individual joined in union with Christ that the Christian believer is adopted into the family of God. *The inseparability of the union undergirds and guarantees the indissolubility of the adoption.* To designate in an alternative way the relations involved, two things can be said. First, the grace of adoption means that the member of the family now lives under a new Fatherhood, from whose grace all of the blessings of adoption flow. And second, that membership carries with it, as has been seen, a vital union with the Son who has been designated Head of the family. An expansive connotation of the union and adoption is contained in chapters 12 of the Westminster Confession of Faith (1647), the Savoy Declaration of Faith (1658), and the Second London (Baptist) Confession (1689).[12]

Fourth, the union with Christ together with adoption means that, as the confessions state, the individual members are, as a result, "never cast off, but sealed to the day of redemption, and inherit the promises, as heirs of everlasting life."

But it should be noted that the confessions we have referred to not only state that "the children of God have his name put upon them, receive the Spirit of adoption, have access to the throne of grace with boldness, are enabled to cry Abba, Father, are pitied, protected, provided for." The

---

11. à Brakel, op. cit, vol. 2, 89.
12. Those three confessions contain identically worded chapters 12.

equally relevant statement is made, sobering in its significance, that such persons are "chastened by him as a Father." But why the chastening? we might ask. And the answer takes us to the remaining issue that we have already anticipated. The chastening, to put it in shortest terms, necessarily follows from the fact of sin in the life of the Christian believer. It is at that point, to state the issue again, that we have the paradox of faith in the Christian life. The paradox resides in the fact, we have said, that the adopted member of the family of God is both a saint and a sinner. We look, then, at some aspects of the meaning of what is involved in that realization.

THE ADOPTED LIFE

At this point the twofold issues we raised at the beginning, those of both the *soteriological* and the *epistemological* aspects of God's revelation and purpose, are directly relevant. We recall, then, the point at which we began and consider the light it throws on the matter of the progress, and, as we are now confronting it, the elements of sin within that progress, in the adopted Christian's life. When we raised the issues of soteriology and epistemology, of the method of salvation on the one hand and the competence and validity of knowledge on the other, we saw something of the relations between them. We found, to restate our principal conclusion, that the questions of both salvation (soteriology) and knowledge (epistemology) are resolved in Christ. Salvation exists alone in his perfect substitutionary life and work; and all criteria of knowledge and truth reside in him. The latter question of what and how we can possibly know comes markedly into focus now as we consider the Christian believer's walk in faith. Let me put what is involved in the following terms.

We know God because God has fulfilled his promise, "I will give them an heart to know me, that I am the Lord: and they shall be my people, and I will be their God" (Jer 24:7). Recalling our earlier comment on the possibility of knowing God, we know him because, firstly, he has made a clear propositional revelation of who he is and what his purposes are with relation to us and our proper relation to him; secondly, that objective revelation is accompanied by his Spirit's renewing work within the human soul that endows the very capacity to know; and thirdly, that endowment of soul carries with it a disposition, or *habitus*, that with a new naturalness seeks after God. While God's propositional revelation is clear, it remains unassimilable to the mind of the man who is not yet the subject of God's renewing grace. God's *objective* revelation is communicated to us by reason of the Spirit-established *subjective* knowledge capacity and the new disposition within the soul.

But two aspects of our life follow from that initiative which God by his grace has instituted. On the one hand, and allowing the focus of thought to fall firstly on the blessings in the life lived within the compass of God's adoption, it is true that "Eye hath not seen, nor ear heard, neither have entered into the heart of man, the things which God hath prepared for them that love him" (1 Cor 2:9). The exegesis of the text might lead us to believe that what is in view in it refers to the prospect that God has prepared for his people when they finally have access to the day of glory. Or it might be thought that the reference is to the darkness of mind of the unregenerate man who is unable to see or glimpse or understand what God is doing with and for the people he has redeemed. That possible exegesis of the text might be reinforced by the further statement in the same context that "the natural man receiveth not the things of the Spirit of God: for they are foolishness unto him: neither can he know them, because they are spiritually discerned" (1 Cor 2:14). But the principal focus of the apostle's argument has reference, we may conclude, to the fact that the believer does not know, and has not been able to contemplate or imagine, what blessings God has stored up for him *in this life*. The reference, in other words, is to the walk of faith in this life. As to the question again of what we do or can know, it is simply true that God has hidden in his purposes for us more than we can contemplate or imagine, let alone know. It is true, as the text goes on to say, that "God has revealed [those things] unto us by his Spirit" (1 Cor 2:10). But to say that the revelation that is thereby received is complete, entire, and comprehensive, and that it takes up all that resides in the mind of God as to the glory of it and the eternally significant interrelations within it, would fly in the face of all we have argued regarding the partialness of the knowledge that God by his Spirit imparts to us. It remains true for the Christian in his walk in this life that he simply does not know, and he cannot know, all that God has laid up and ordained for him, either in this life or in that which is to come.

A second aspect of the adopted life warrants reflection. Because we live in ignorance of God's purpose in what he has planned for us in the days that are yet to come, we live, therefore, in trust and faith in his providential ordering. In that respect, we don't know, because we cannot know, because what is yet to come is hidden from us. But life in that condition of ignorance and the impossibility of knowing does not detract from our settled confidence in God, into whose family we have been adopted. We know, where we cannot see, that he is making "all things work together for good" (Rom 8:28). That is the measure of our trust. The apostle Peter addressed that condition when he said, referring to our relation to Christ with whom we are joined in union: "Whom having not seen, ye love; in whom, though now ye see him not, yet believing, ye rejoice with joy unspeakable and full of glory" (1 Pet 1:8).

But our immediate concern probes beyond the level of the blessings that life in the adopted family of God provides. We are concerned with what the confessions we have referred to have noted as the chastisement of God the Father. That, we said, issues from the wandering sinfulness of which we are all too easily capable, even though we are true, and truly adopted, believers. We turn finally to reflect on what is involved in that connection.

Again, and most significantly, the question of knowledge and ignorance comes into focus at this point. We refer first to what is perhaps the most alarming aspect of what is now in view. We take this point of relevance first because of the significance it has for the Christian believer's probe into the meaning of sin. It has been addressed by the Psalmist when he prayed: "[C]leanse thou me from my secret faults" (Ps 19:12). At that point David is concerned and worried about the all too real possibility that, while he lived in the presence of God and before his all-seeing eyes, he was guilty of sin of which he himself had not been aware. That is the issue raised by the Psalmist's insightful recognition that in our Christian walk our very sensitivity to sin, or, we may say, our lack of sensitivity, may leave us unaware of what sin really is and means. Moses also, in his Psalm, evinces similar insight when he observes that "Thou hast set our iniquities before thee, our *secret sins* in the light of thy countenance" (Ps 90:8). The commentator, Matthew Poole, rightly refers to "secret faults" as "such sins as were secret . . . from myself; such as I never observed, or did not discern the evil of." And Poole continues, "Pardon my unknown sins, of which I never repented particularly, as I should have done."[13] Spurgeon is not wide of the mark when he concludes that "We have but a very few sins which we can observe and detect, compared with those which are hidden from

---

13. Poole, *Commentary*, at Ps. 19:12.

ourselves."[14] It is no wonder that the old seventeenth-century Puritan, Ralph Venning, saw sin as "the plague of plagues."[15]

But the meaning of the possibility of *secret sins*, connoted in the respect we have stated, has a number of implications for the Christian believer's walk in faith. First, why should there be within the Christian's life-journey any secret sin? The answer turns again on a lack of knowledge. But the fact and the meaning of that lack needs to be worked out a little more fully. The prophet Hosea has illuminated an aspect of what is involved in conveying God's complaint that "My people are destroyed for lack of knowledge" (Hos 4:6). But then the same prophet reflects on the antidote of the ignorance of which he had complained when he said: "Then we shall know, if we follow on to know the Lord" (Hos 6:3). So that, at a minimum level, the sins of which we are guilty occur because we have not cultivated the presence of God as we might have done. We have not cultivated the habit of assiduous attention to the mandates of his word and the imperatives of the morality to which his law alerts us. We have not been careful to cultivate an understanding of the real meaning of the status to which we have been raised by reason of our union with Christ; and we have not attended as we should to the imperatives which that status carries with it. Lamentably, though we are God's people who have been adopted into the membership of his family, the reality is that we know him only slightly, and we know only slightly what should be the penetrating and calming wholeness of his preceptive law. We have not learned well the import of the Psalmist's confession that "I have set the Lord always before me: because he is at my right hand, I shall not be moved" (Ps 16:8).

The antidote is that we should seek to practice more effectively the presence of God. Do we not yet know what our Lord himself invited us to, the feast of his presence, when he said "Behold, I stand at the door and knock: if any man hear my voice, and open the door, I will come in to him, and will sup with him, and he with me" (Rev 3:20)? Christ's invitation to us to let him into our hearts has to do with our enjoyment of the blessing of his sanctifying grace that he waits to communicate to us. It is a call to diligence in cultivating the presence of God.

---

14. Spurgeon, *Treasury of David*, vol. 1, 275.
15. Venning, *Plague of Plagues*.

But there is further reason for secret sin. Again it has to do with lack of knowledge, and a proper understanding of it points to the wonder of the grace of God in the Christian believer's progressive sanctification. The fact needs to be faced that at various stages of one's walk in the life of faith, perhaps notably at an early stage, one may naturally engage in actions, manner of life, and cultural accommodations that are in themselves sinful in the light of God's preceptive mandates. But at the stage of spiritual maturity that then exists, those indulgences are not understood or recognized as sin. One then sins the sin of ignorance. The sins are secret, in the sense in which we have seen such sin to be operative, in that they are not recognized as sin and the believer is therefore not aware of their import and their guilt. As in the case of the Psalmist, they are therefore unrepented. But as in the Psalmist's case again, the believer's advancing sensitivity will cause him to plead with God for the forgiveness of whatever unwitting sin has been placed to his account. For that also, though the import and significance of it may at the time be lost to the individual's consciousness, has been covered by the imputed righteousness of Christ.

Sin, then, is complex. Sin is, clearly, a transgression of the law of God (1 John 3:4). On another view, sin is whatever in thought, word, or deed outrages the holiness of God. Sin is, at the most fundamental level, the repudiation of covenantal obligations that we sustain to God. It is the assertion of autonomy in the face of God, the supposition that we can live in terms of criteria of belief and action that we excogitate from within ourselves or extract from the cultural milieu in which we live. Sin is, in its final expression, a love of self rather than a love of God.

But more than the secret sin, the sin of ignorance, tarnishes the Christian's life and walk. Equally damning, if not more so, is the sin of which we are guilty, consciously guilty, while at the same time we claim the privileges of adoption into membership of the family of God. Is it never the case that we dally with what, in our better moments, we know clearly to be sin? It is undoubtedly true, dangerously true, that there is pleasure in sin. Has the child of God never been shocked into painful awareness that he has fallen where he should have been "stedfast, immoveable" (1 Cor 15:58)? Have we never been startlingly awakened to the fact that "Satan himself is transformed into an angel of light" (2 Cor 11:14) and that he is able for a time to "deceive the very elect"? Have we never been so sure of our ability to walk circumspectly in the way of righteousness that our very self-reliance has brought us to the agony of fall and defeat? But if we are realistic enough to agree that sin may well be for a time pleasurable, consider Moses of whom it is said that he chose "rather to suffer affliction with the people of God, than to enjoy the pleasures of sin for a season." And the reason, in its starkest simplicity, was that he "esteem[ed] the reproach of Christ greater riches than the treasures in Egypt: for he had respect unto the recompense of the reward" (Heb 11:25–26). The antidote to the ensnaring appearances of the pleasures of sin has been stated definitively in Moses' reaction.

What all of the foregoing amounts to is that our adoption into the family of God and our consciousness of the high implications of our union with Christ beckon us to the cultivation of an increasing sensitivity to the sinfulness of sin. How we should mourn with the poet of the evangelical awakening, William Cowper, when he says that he "hate[s] the sins that made thee [Christ] mourn, And drove thee from my breast."[16] We have already observed the expression of our Puritan fathers that it is the most advanced saint who is most conscious of the sinfulness of sin and of the blackness of his own heart.

CONCLUSION

We have spoken, briefly but sufficiently for our present purposes, of the realities of the Christian believer's union with Christ and his adoption into the family of God. A number of implications of what has been said can be summarized.

First, all of our felicity as believers, and all of our comfort in this life and our hope for that which is to come, are found in Christ. God has made him to be unto us "wisdom, and righteousness, and sanctification, and redemption" (1 Cor 1:30). Fullness of life abides only in him to whom we are joined in an indissoluble union. Christ alone is "the way, the truth, and the life" (John 14:6), and the Christian's heart desire is to glory in nothing "save in the cross of our Lord Jesus Christ" (Gal 6:14). As Christ came "that he might deliver us from this present evil world" (Gal 1:4), he now demands, and by his grace we determine to give him, our totalitarian allegiance. It is in Christ that what we have seen as the soteriological and the epistemological questions are resolved.

Second, we know that in the life-journey of righteousness on which God has established us we shall arrive at last at the inheritance he has pre-

---

16. Davie, *New Oxford Book of Christian Verse*, 198.

pared for us (Heb 9:15). For has Christ himself not said that "if I go and prepare a place for you, I will come again, and receive you unto myself; that where I am there ye may be also" (John 14:2–3)? In our life-journey our dependence is totally upon him. Our histories are in his hands. We cannot yet see all of the way. We cannot know his purpose and our way as he knows. We live, nevertheless, in trust upon him because we live in ignorance of what he has prepared for us. In that life of trust we know that the history he is working out for us is linear, its projection is upward. Our history is not confined to a circular blankness and ignorance. Of course, the upward journey is not without its interruptions that are due to the failures of sin, both sins of ignorance and sins of volition. But though the temporary swings of guilt and grace occur, our gaze, in the better moments to which God repeatedly, again and again, recalls us, is on the Savior whose we are and to whom we will come at last.

Finally, what need is there for anything or anyone else than Christ who has redeemed us when, as the apostle has said, "[Y]e are complete in him" (Col 2:10)? May we yet learn to serve him more faithfully, to walk with him more closely, and to honor him in all things more completely.

Bibliography

à Brakel, Wilhelmus. *The Christian's Reasonable Service*. Translated by Bartel Elshout. Grand Rapids: Reformation Heritage Books, vol. 1, 1992.
———. *The Christian's Reasonable Service*. Translated by Bartel Elshout. Grand Rapids: Reformation Heritage Books, vol. 2, 1993.
Abrams, M. H., editor. *The Norton Anthology of English Literature*. New York: Norton, 1962.
Alderson, Richard. *No Holiness, No Heaven*. Edinburgh: Banner of Truth, 1986.
Anselm. *Monologium and Proslogium: With the Replies of Gaunilo and Anselm*. Translated by Thomas Wilson. Indianapolis, IN: Hackett Publishing, 1996.
Arand, Charles P. "The Church's Dogma and Biblical Theology." In *A Confessing Theology for Postmodern Times*, edited by Michael S. Horton, 15–27. Wheaton: Crossway Books, 2000.
Armstrong, John H. *The Coming Evangelical Crisis: Challenges to the Authority of Scripture and the Gospel*. Chicago: Moody Press, 1996.
Auber, Harriet. *Our Blest Redeemer, ere He breathed His tender, last farewell*. In Congregational Praise, 209.
Augustine. *Confessions*. Translated by Henry Chadwick. Oxford: Oxford University Press, 1991.
Bahnsen, Greg L. *Van Til's Apologetics: Readings and Analysis*. Phillipsburg, NJ: P&R Publishing, 1998.
Bavinck, Herman. *Reformed Dogmatics: Volume 3: Sin and Salvation in Christ*. Translated by John Vriend. Grand Rapids: Baker Academic, 2006.
———. *Reformed Dogmatics: Volume 4: Holy Spirit, Church, and New Creation*. Translated by John Vriend. Grand Rapids: Baker Academic, 2008.
———. *The Doctrine of God*. Translated by William Hendriksen. Edinburgh: Banner of Truth, 1977.
Beale, G. K. and James Bibza. "The New Testament: The Covenant of Redemption in Jesus Christ." In *Building a Christian World View*, edited by W. Andrew Hoffecker, 49–70. Phillipsburg, NJ: P&R Publishing, 1986.
Beeke, Joel. R and Sinclair B. Ferguson, editors. *Reformed Confessions Harmonized*. Grand Rapids: Baker Books, 1999.
Berkhof, L. *Systematic Theology*. Grand Rapids: Eerdmans, 1939.
Blamires, Harry. *Recovering the Christian Mind: Meeting the Challenge of Secularism*. Downers Grove: InterVarsity Press, 1988.
———. *The Christian Mind: How Should A Christian Think*. London: Society for the Promotion of Christian Knowledge, 1963. Reprint Ann Arbor, MI: Servant Books, 1978.

———. *The PostChristian Mind: Exposing its Destructive Agenda.* Ann Arbor, MI: Servant Publications, 1999.

Blanchard, John. *Does God believe in atheists?* Darlington, UK: Evangelical Press, 2000.

Boston, Thomas. *Human Nature in its Fourfold State.* London: Banner of Truth, 1964.

Calvin, John. *Institutes of the Christian Religion.* Edited by John T. McNeill. Translated by Ford Lewis Battles. 2 vols. Philadelphia: Westminster Press, 1960.

Cherry, Conrad. *The Theology of Jonathan Edwards: A Reappraisal.* Bloomington: Indiana University Press, 1990.

Clark, R. Scott, editor. *Covenant, Justification, and Pastoral Ministry: Essays by the faculty of Westminster Seminary California.* Phillipsburg, NJ: P&R Publishing, 2007.

Clifford, Alan C. *Atonement and Justification: English Evangelical Theology 1640–1790: An Evaluation.* Oxford: Clarendon Press, 1990.

Congregational Praise (hymnal). London: Independent Press, for the Congregational Union of England and Wales, 1951.

Cowper, William. *God moves in a mysterious way.* In Trinity Hymnal, 128, and various hymnals.

Craig, William Lane. *The Only Wise God.* Grand Rapids: Baker, 1987.

Cunningham, William. *Historical Theology.* 2 vols. London: Banner of Truth, 1960.

———. *The Reformers and the Theology of the Reformation.* London: Banner of Truth, 1967.

Dabney, Robert L. *Discussions: Evangelical and Theological.* 2 vols. London: Banner of Truth, 1967.

———. *Lectures in Systematic Theology.* Grand Rapids: Zondervan, 1972.

Davie, Donald, editor. *The New Oxford Book of Christian Verse.* Oxford: Oxford University Press, 1981.

Descartes, René. *Discourse on Method and the Meditations on First Philosophy.* Translated by Donald A. Cress. Indianapolis, IN: Hackett Publishing, 1998.

Edwards, Jonathan. *An Inquiry into . . . Freedom of the Will.* Morgan, PA: Soli Deo Gloria Publications, 1996.

———. *Freedom of the Will.* Edited by Paul Ramsey. New Haven: Yale University Press, 1957.

———. *The Works of Jonathan Edwards.* Edited by Edward Hickman. 2 vols. London: Ball, Arnold and Co., 1840.

Fee, Gordon D. *The First Epistle to the Corinthians.* Grand Rapids: Eerdmans, 1987.

Ferguson, Sinclair. *John Owen on the Christian Life.* Edinburgh: Banner of Truth, 1987.

———. *The Holy Spirit.* Downers Grove: InterVarsity, 1996.

Flavel, John. "The Method of Grace in the Gospel Redemption." In John Flavel. *The Works of John Flavel.* 6 vols. London: Banner of Truth, 1968.

Frame, John. *No Other God: A Response to Open Theism.* Phillipsburg, NJ: P&R Publishing, 2001.

———. *The Doctrine of God.* Phillipsburg, NJ: P&R Publishing, 2002.

———. *The Doctrine of the Knowledge of God.* Phillipsburg, NJ: P&R Publishing, 1987.

Gaffin, Richard B. Jr. *"By Faith, not by Sight": Paul and the Order of Salvation.* Milton Keynes, UK: Paternoster, 2006.

———. *Resurrection and Redemption.* Phillipsburg, NJ: P&R Publishing, 1987.

Garcia, Mark A. "Imputation and the Christology of Union with Christ: Calvin, Osziander, and the Contemporary Quest for a Reformed Model." *Westminster Theological Journal,* 68 (2006) 219–51.

———. "Review Article: No Reformed Theology of Justification?" (Containing a review of *Covenant, Justification, and Pastoral Ministry*, edited by R. Scott Clark). Orthodox Presbyterian Church: *Ordained Servant* (October, 2007). No pages. Online: http://www.opc.org/os9.html.

Geehan, E. R., editor. *Jerusalem and Athens: Critical Discussions on the Theology and Apologetics of Cornelius Van Til.* Philadelphia: Presbyterian and Reformed, 1971.

Godfrey, W. Robert and David VanDrunen. "Response to Mark Garcia's review of *Covenant, Justification and Pastoral Ministry*." Orthodox Presbyterian Church: *Ordained Servant* (December, 2007). No pages. Online: http://www.opc.org/os9.html.

Hägglund, Bengt. *History of Theology.* Translated by Gene J. Lund. St. Louis: Concordia Publishing House, 1968.

Harnack, Adolf. *History of Dogma.* 7 vols. Translated by James Millar. New York: Dover, 1951.

———. *Outlines of the History of Dogma.* Translated by E. K. Mitchell. Boston: Beacon Press, 1957.

Helm, Paul. *Calvin and the Calvinists.* Edinburgh: Banner of Truth, 1982.

———. *Eternal God: A Study of God without Time.* Oxford: Clarendon Press, 1988.

———. *The Providence of God.* Downers Grove: InterVarsity, 1993.

Hendriksen, William. *New Testament Commentary: Exposition of the Gospel According to John.* Grand Rapids: Baker Books, 1954.

Henley, William Ernest. *Invictus.* Online: http://www.bartleby.com/103/7.html, and various editions.

Henry, Matthew. *An Exposition of the Old and New Testaments.* Various editions.

Hodge, A. A. *Outlines of Theology.* Edinburgh: Banner of Truth, 1972.

Hodge, Charles. *Commentary on 1 & 2 Corinthians.* Edinburgh: Banner of Truth, 1974.

———. *Systematic Theology.* 4 vols. London: Thomas Nelson, 1873.

Hoffecker, W. Andrew, editor. *Building a Christian World View.* Phillipsburg: P&R Publishing, 1986.

Horton, Michael S. *Covenant and Salvation: Union with Christ.* Louisville: Westminster John Knox Press. 2007.

———, editor. *A Confessing Theology for Postmodern Times.* Wheaton: Crossway Books, 2000.

Kant, Immanuel. *Critique of Pure Reason.* Translated by F. Max Miller. New York: Macmillan, 1966.

Karlberg, Mark. "On the Theological Correlation of Divine and Human Language: A Review Article." *Journal of the Evangelical Theological Society* 32/1 (1989) 99–105.

Kendall, R. T. *Calvin and English Calvinism To 1649.* Oxford: Oxford University Press, 1979.

Kuyper, Abraham. *Principles of Sacred Theology.* Translated by J. Hendrik de Vries. Grand Rapids: Eerdmans, 1963.

Luther, Martin. *The Bondage of the Will.* Translated by J. I. Packer and O. R. Johnston. Westwood, NJ: Fleming Revell, 1957.

Malcolm, Norman. "Malcolm's Statement of Anselm's Ontological Argument." In *The Ontological Argument*, edited by Alvin Plantinga, 146. Garden City: Anchor, 1965.

Milton, John. *Paradise Lost.* In M. H. Abrams, editor. *The Norton Anthology of English Literature*, 452.

Murray, John. *Collected Writings of John Murray.* Edinburgh: Banner of Truth, vol. 2, 1977.

———. *Redemption—Accomplished and Applied*. Grand Rapids: Eerdmans, 1955.
———. *The Epistle to the Romans*. 2 vols. Grand Rapids: Eerdmans, 1959.
———. *The Imputation of Adam's Sin*. Grand Rapids: Eerdmans, 1959.
Naugle, David K. *Worldview: The History of a Concept*. Grand Rapids: Eerdmans, 2002.
Nicene Creed. In Trinity Hymnal, 846, and various editions.
Nicoll, W. Robertson, editor. *The Expositor's Greek Testament*. Grand Rapids: Eerdmans, vol. 4. Reprint 1979.
Noll, Mark A. *The Scandal of the Evangelical Mind*. Grand Rapids: Eerdmans, 1994.
———. *Turning Points: Decisive Moments in the History of Christianity*. 2d ed. Grand Rapids: Baker, 2000.
Oliphint, K. Scott, editor. *Justified In Christ: God's plan for us in Justification*. Fearn, Scotland: Christian Focus Publications, Mentor Imprint, 2007.
Owen, John. *The Death of Death in the Death of Christ*. London: Banner of Truth, 1959.
———. *The Works of John Owen*. Edinburgh: Banner of Truth, vol. 3, 1965.
———. *The Works of John Owen*. Edinburgh: Banner of Truth, vol. 6, 1967.
Plantinga, Alvin, editor. *The Ontological Argument: From St. Anselm to Contemporary Philosophers*. Garden City: Anchor, 1965.
Poole, Matthew. *A Commentary on the Holy Bible*. 3 vols. London: Banner of Truth, 1962.
Reymond, Robert L. *A New Systematic Theology of the Christian Faith*. Nashville: Thomas Nelson, 1998.
Ridderbos, Herman. *Paul: An Outline of His Theology*. Translated by John Richard de Witt. Grand Rapids: Eerdmans, 1975.
Savoy Declaration of Faith. 1658. Various editions.
Schaff, Philip. *History of the Christian Church*. 8 vols. Grand Rapids: Eerdmans, 1910.
Second London (Baptist) Confession. 1689. Various editions.
Shedd, W.G.T. *A History of Christian Doctrine*. 2 vols. New York: Charles Scribner's Sons, 1868.
———. *Dogmatic Theology*. 3 vols. New York: Charles Scribner's Sons, 1888–94. Reprint Grand Rapids: Zondervan, n.d.
Small, James. *I've found a friend, O such a friend*. In Trinity Hymnal, 517, and various hymnals.
Sproul, R. C. *Faith Alone: The Evangelical Doctrine of Justification*. Grand Rapids: Baker Books, 1995.
Sproul, R. C., et al. *Classical Apologetics: A Rational Defense of the Christian Faith and a Critique of Presuppositional Apologetics*. Grand Rapids: Zondervan, 1984.
Spurgeon, C. H. *The Treasury of David*. McLean, VA: Macdonald Publishing, n.d.
Strimple, Robert B. "What Does God Know?" In *The Coming Evangelical Crisis*, edited by John H. Armstrong, 140–41. Chicago: Moody Press, 1996.
Thiselton, Anthony C. *The First Epistle to the Corinthians: A Commentary on the Greek Text*. Grand Rapids: Eerdmans, 2000.
Tipton, Lane G. "Union with Christ and Justification." In *Justified in Christ: God's plan for us in Justification*, edited by K. Scott Oliphint, 23–49. Fearn, Scotland: Christian Focus Publications, Mentor Imprint, 2007.
———, and Jeffrey C. Waddington, editors. *Resurrection and Eschatology: Theology in Service of the Church: Essays in Honor of Richard B. Gaffin, Jr.* Phillipsburg, NJ: P&R Publishing, 2008.
Trinity Hymnal. Atlanta: Great Commission Publications, 1990.

Turretin, Francis. *Institutes of Elenctic Theology, Volume 1*. Translated by George Musgrave Ciger. Phillipsburg, NJ: P&R Publishing, 1992.

———. *Institutes of Elenctic Theology, Volume 2*. Translated by George Musgrave Giger. Phillipsburg, NJ: P&R Publishing, 1994.

Vande Kapelle, Robert P. and John D. Currid, "The Old Testament: The Covenant Between God and Man." In *Building a Christian World View*, edited by W. Andrew Hoffecker, 11–48. Phillipsburg, NJ: P&R Publishing, 1986.

VanDrunen, David. "The Two Kingdoms and the *ordo salutis*: Life Beyond Judgment and the Question of a Dual Ethic." *The Westminster Theological Journal* 70, 2 (2008) 207–224.

Van Til, Cornelius. *A Christian Theory of Knowledge*. Philadelphia: Presbyterian and Reformed, 1969.

———. *An Introduction to Systematic Theology*. Philadelphia: Presbyterian and Reformed, 1974.

———. *Common Grace*. Philadelphia: Presbyterian and Reformed, 1954.

———. *The Defense of the Faith*. Philadelphia: Presbyterian and Reformed, 1963.

———. *The Reformed Pastor and Modern Thought*. Philadelphia: Presbyterian and Reformed, 1971.

Venning, Ralph. *The Plague of Plagues*. London: Banner of Truth, 1965.

Vickers, Douglas. *Christian Confession and the Crackling Thorn*. Grand Rapids: Reformation Heritage Books, 2004.

———. *Divine Redemption and the Refuge of Faith*. Grand Rapids: Reformation Heritage Books, 2005.

———. *The Fracture of Faith: Recovering belief of the gospel in a postmodern world*. Fearn, Scotland: Christian Focus Publications, Mentor Imprint, 2000.

———. *The Texture of Truth*. Grand Rapids: Reformation Heritage Books, 2007.

———. *When God Converts a Sinner*. Eugene, OR: Wipf & Stock, 2008.

Vos, Geerhardus. *The Pauline Eschatology*. Grand Rapids: Eerdmans, 1961.

Weeks, Noel. *The Sufficiency of Scripture*. Edinburgh: Banner of Truth, 1988.

Wenger, Thomas L., "The New Perspective on Calvin: Responding to Recent Calvin Interpretations." *Journal of the Evangelical Theological Society* 50 (2007) 311–28.

Westminster Confession of Faith. 1647. Various editions.

Westminster Shorter Catechism. 1647. Various editions.

White, Newport J. D. *Commentary on the First and Second Epistles to Timothy*. In W. Robertson Nicoll, editor. *The Expositor's Greek Testament*, vol. 4, 119. Grand Rapids: Eerdmans, 1979.

Witsius, Herman. *The Economy of the Covenants Between God and Man*. 2 vols. Translated by William Crookshank. Phillipsburg, NJ: P&R Publishing for the den Dulk Christian Foundation, 1990.

Wright, R. K. McGregor. *No Place for Sovereignty: What's Wrong with Freewill Theism*. Downers Grove: InterVarsity Press, 1996.

Young, Edward J. *Studies in Genesis One*. Philadelphia: Presbyterian and Reformed, 1964.

———. *The Book of Isaiah*. 3 vols. Grand Rapids: Eerdmans, 1972.

www.ingramcontent.com/pod-product-compliance
Lightning Source LLC
Chambersburg PA
CBHW070918180426
43192CB00038B/1750